SANS Step-by-Step Series

COMPUTER SECURITY INCIDENT HANDLING

An Action Plan for Dealing with Intrusions, Cyber-Theft, and Other Security-Related Events

Version 2.3.1

March 2003

Stephen Northcutt

Document Legalities

Managing Editor: Barbara H. Rietveld
Publication Designer: José Ellauri
International Standard Book Number: 0-9724273-7-6
Library of Congress Control Number: 2003103826
Printed in the United States of America

Warning and Disclaimer

A WORD FROM SANS INCIDENT HANDLING PROGRAM DIRECTOR

Incident handling is similar to emergency medicine. The caregiver tends to be under pressure, and mistakes can be very costly. A simple, well understood approach is best. This is why even the most experienced incident handling experts follow well defined and systematic procedures for responding to security-related incidents. They keep the six stages (preparation, detection, containment, eradication, recovery, and follow-up) in mind; they use predesigned forms; and they call on others for help.

Few individuals have sufficient incident handling experience to provide guidance for all types of incidents and for all types of organizations. The guide reflects the experience of incident handlers from more than 50 organizations: commercial, government, and educational. In addition, two of the most respected incident handling organizations brought their cumulative experience to the effort.

Please use this guide as a starting point to create a set of incident handling procedures tailored to your organization's environment. As you work through the preparation tasks, ask yourself, "If an incident occurred, would I be really thankful if I had done that?" and in the response sections ask, "Would I be really sorry if I hadn't done that?"

If you are in a very small organization, implement the parts of this guide that you can afford. Whatever the size of your organization, please let us know of errors or omissions. We'll be reissuing the guide periodically. Email suggestions to <info@sans.org>, using the subject "Incident Handling Guide."

When an incident occurs, don't hurry!

I still remember responding to my first alert after earning my Emergency Medical Technician (EMT) certification. My pager went off and I was flying. I zoomed right by this old geezer, who happened to be an assistant fire chief and paramedic with decades of experience. He reached out with a meaty hand and stopped me in my tracks. "Slow down," he said in a gruff voice. "Even if you don't hurt yourself or someone else running like that, when you get there you won't be any good to anyone panting and wheezing." A decade and a half later, I am the old geezer, and I want to pass the same advice on to you. Especially with your first few incidents, slow down. Take time to take notes. Notice and appreciate the work of others on the team. Be as kind as you can under difficult circumstances.

Finally, if your organization's policy will allow it, share what you have learned with other incident handlers and computer incident response (CIRT) teams. Attacks against computers are happening everywhere, all the time, and the attackers are in constant communication. Coordinating your efforts with those of other teams is a critical facet of successful incident response. Do as they told you to do in kindergarten: Share.

Stephen Northcutt
SANS Institute

This document is the joint product of computer security professionals from corporations, government agencies, and educational institutions. They carry battle scars from more incident handling experiences than many would like to remember.

SANS Institute enthusiastically applauds the work of these professionals and their willingness to share the lessons they have learned and the techniques they use.

Contributing authors and reviewers on this updated version

Greg Jones, Consultant
Steve Weil, Seitel Leeds and Associates
Robert Ashworth, US CENTCOM
Adrien de Beaupré, Elytra Enterprises Inc.
Marvin Marin, EDS
Jerry Patterson, Comcast IP Services Inc.
Brian Stewart, Schlumberger

Supporting authors and reviewers on prior editions

AusCERT, The Australian Computer Emergency Response Team
Bryce Alexander, The Vanguard Group
S. Dirk Anderson, Frontier ConferTech
Connie Balodimos, BankBoston
Larry Bassett, FORE Systems Inc.
Dave Bixler, Mount Abora Consulting
Sean Boran, Boran Consulting
Peter Brantley, University of California, San Francisco
John J. Brassil, Vanderbilt University
Jeffrey W. Brown
Chris Calabrese, BFR Systems
Brian Carrier @Stake
Laura Carriere, Raytheon STX
Jeff Davis, Lucent Technologies
George Dimitoglou, Space Applications Corporation
Dennis J. Duval, Epic USA
Nicki A. Eger, US Department of Defense
Andy Feldt, University of Oklahoma
Robert G. Ferrell, US Geological Survey
David Goldberg, The MITRE Corporation
Michael Gregorio, The Coca-Cola Company
Kenneth L. Grossman, Federal Computer Incident Response Center
Tom Gutnick, Data General Corporation
Larry Hale, Federal Computer Incident Response Center
Paul Herrmann, P.I., eVestigations
Theresa Ho, Lucent Technologies
Kent Landfield, Network Flight Recorder
James Kane III, Information Network of Arkansas
Yaron Keshet, P.S. Publishing
William J. Maciura, Tec Voc High School
Eric Maiwald, Fortrex Technologies
Jeffrey E. Man, Nichols Research Corporation
Rob Marchand, Array Systems Computing
Brian Martin, RepSec
John Mason, Hughes Aircraft Employees Federal Credit Union
Chris Mc Donald, White Sands Missile Range
David A. McGuire, Information Security Systems
Michael Mietlicki, Thomson Financial
James H. Moore, Xerox Corporation
Kathleen M. Moriarty, FactSet Research Systems
Kathleen M. Padgett, Los Alamos National Laboratory
A. Padgett Peterson, Lockheed-Martin Corporation
Dennis Poindexter, US Ballistic Missile Defense Organization
Ralph A. Rodriguez, Treacy & Company
Ben Schmitz, Fastparts
Michael T Shinn, Cisco Systems
Andres J. Silva III, Ameritech
Ken Smith, Interliant Inc.
Donald J. Smith, General Dynamics
John C. Smith, Prevention and Recovery Solutions
Sandy Sparks, CIAC, The Computer Incident Advisory Capability of the US Department of Energy
Aurobindo Sundaram, Schlumberger
Saul Tannenbaum, Tufts University
Aron Thomas, Pacific Gas & Electric
Stephen Tihor, New York University
Scott A. West, American Express
Paul G. Williams, United States Air Force
Nigel Willson, Disney Online
Lenny Zeltser
Laurie Zirkle, Virginia Tech

TABLE OF CONTENTS

THE EMERGENCY ACTION CARD

When a computer security incident occurs and you are not prepared, follow these nine steps:

- **Emergency Step 1.** Remain calm. Even a fairly mild incident tends to raise everyone's stress level. Communication and coordination become difficult. Your composure can help others avoid making critical errors.

- **Emergency Step 2.** Take good notes. Use the forms in the back of this guide. Start with the one titled "Incident Identification." Then work your way through the others that are relevant. As you complete the forms, keep in mind that your notes may become evidence in court. Make sure you answer the four W's: Who, What, When, Where and for extra credit, How and Why. You may find a small hand-held tape recorder to be a valuable tool.

- **Emergency Step 3.** Notify the right people and get help. Begin by notifying your security coordinator and your manager. Ask that a co-worker be assigned to help coordinate the incident handling process. Get a copy of the corporate phonebook and keep it with you. Ask your helper to keep careful notes on each person with whom he or she has spoken and what was said. Make sure you do the same.

- **Emergency Step 4.** Enforce a "need to know" policy. Tell the details of the incident to the minimum number of people possible. Remind them, where appropriate, that they are trusted individuals and that your organization is counting on their discretion. Avoid speculation except when it is required to decide what to do. Too often, the initial information in an incident is misinterpreted and the "working theory" has to be scrapped.

- **Emergency Step 5.** Use out of band communications. If the computers have been compromised, avoid using them for incident handling discussions. Use telephones and faxes instead. Do not send information about the incident by electronic mail, talk, chat, or news; the information may be intercepted by the attacker and used to worsen the situation. When computers are being used, encrypt all incident handling e-mail.

- **Emergency Step 6.** Contain the problem. Take the necessary steps to keep the problem from getting worse. Usually that means removing the system from the network, though management may decide to keep the connections open in an effort to catch an intruder.

- **Emergency Step 7.** Make a backup of the affected system(s) as soon as is practicable. Use new, unused media. If possible make a binary, or bit-by-bit backup. Tools like SafeBack or, in a pinch, Norton Ghost can execute binary backups on Intel platforms. If you have time to learn the tool "dd" before the incident, it is available for both Unix and Windows and has been used in cases that went to court a number of times, but it does take practice.

- **Emergency Step 8.** Get rid of the problem. Identify what went wrong if you can. Take steps to correct the deficiencies that allowed the problem to occur.

- **Emergency Step 9.** Get back in business. After checking your backups to ensure they are not compromised, restore your system from backups, and monitor the system closely to determine whether it can resume its tasks. Monitor the system closely for the next few weeks to ensure it is not compromised again.

- **Emergency Step 10.** Learn from this experience, so you won't get caught unprepared the next time an incident occurs. This guide, *Computer Security Incident Handling,* is designed to help you by providing a systematic approach to incident handling.

INCIDENT HANDLING STEP-BY-STEP

Experienced incident handling professionals divide the process into six phases: preparation, identification, containment, eradication, recovery and follow-up. Understanding these stages, and what can go wrong in each, facilitates a more methodical response, and avoids duplication of effort. It also helps you deal with unexpected aspects of incidents.

PHASE 1. PREPARATION

Problem:* *In the heat of the moment, when an incident has been discovered, rushed decision-making may not be effective. By establishing policies, procedures, and agreements in advance, you minimize the chance of making catastrophic mistakes. Further, by taking proactive measures, you may reduce the number of incidents.

STEP 1.1 USE PROACTIVE TECHNIQUES TO PREVENT INCIDENTS

The best way to "handle" an incident is to stop it from happening in the first place. To do that, you'll need to establish security policies, monitor and analyze the network traffic, enforce a vulnerability patch program, assess vulnerabilities, upgrade the technical security skills of your staff, configure your systems wisely, and establish incident handling training programs. The combination of these tasks makes it more difficult for intruders to access your systems and to harm them if they do.

Action 1.1.1 Patch known system vulnerabilities

The vast majority of computer intrusions occur through well known vulnerabilities. There are no tasks more important in preventing system intrusions than configuring new systems securely and keeping current with vendor security patches. SANS Institute (www.sans.org) publishes, and regularly updates Step-by-Step guides for securing various operating systems including *Windows NT*, *Windows 2000*, *Linux*, and *Solaris*. In addition, SANS publishes free monthly and weekly digests, including the *Security Alert Consensus* and *Critical Vulnerability Analysis* that can help system administrators stay on top of the latest vulnerabilities. These are available from www.sans.org/newsletters. The Center for Internet Security has developed a consensus set of benchmarks that provide prescriptions for minimum security settings (available free at www.cisecurity.org), and the SANS Institute and the National Infrastructure Protection Center at the US Department of Justice have published a consensus list of the top Twenty Internet Security Threats (www.sans.org/top20/) that can help you prioritize your patching efforts. Systems should be regularly audited using the Center for Internet Security tools to ensure patches are in place.

Create a formal process for reviewing security alerts and testing and applying patches. Work with your system administrators to ensure that critical patches are made in the shortest possible time frame. Work patches into your new system-build process so that Internet-facing machines are configured securely before connecting them to the Internet. **NOTE:** One of the lessons from the Code Red worm of July 2001 is that many systems that were behind firewalls also were affected. Many sites now use a standardized build process for so-called bastion hosts (systems that are expected to be Internet facing) as well as for systems that they hope are internal.

Action 1.1.2 Improve technical security skills

In large measure, vulnerabilities are not removed because system and network administrators, and even security professionals, are unaware of the vulnerabilities or do not know what to do about them. In tandem with an aggressive program of vulnerability elimination, it is wise to ask each system and network administrator, as well as every other person who has direct responsibility for system security and operations, to upgrade his or her skills and demonstrate the improvement through certification. The primary certification program for technical security professionals is the Global Information Assurance Certification program, or GIAC. Earning a GIAC certification includes in-depth training, both in live classes or via the Internet, practical exercises to demonstrate mastery, and comprehensive examinations. More information may be found at www.giac.org.

Action 1.1.3 Establish a policy on presumption of privacy

Your organization needs to decide on a policy of presumption of privacy and be willing to enforce that policy. The policy should answer questions such as whether the electronic mail stored on your file server is the property of the organization, or of each individual user of the system. The policy should also establish when encryption is allowed and under what circumstances it is required. The encryption section should cover who keeps the encryption keys, so that disgruntled employees cannot easily encrypt information and then leave.

Action 1.1.4 Post warning banners

From a legal perspective, displaying warning banners is one of the most important steps you can take to prepare for an incident. Every system should display an approved warning banner visible to all users who attempt to login to the system. The banner should state that the system is the property of your organization, is subject to monitoring, and that unauthorized use or access is prohibited. Your legal counsel should review your banner. The banner should not reveal either the operating system or the purpose of the computer.

Action 1.1.5 Establish an organizational approach to incident handling

When an incident is discovered, you will choose between two approaches to incident handling: The first, and generally simplest, is to "contain, clean and deny access." The focus in this approach is to eradicate the problem as quickly as possible and get back into business. The alternative approach, requiring more technical skill and planning, is to "monitor and gather information." Here, you allow the intruder to continue the attack, perhaps with subtle restrictions that minimize further damage. Often, the decision between the two approaches rests on whether you intend to prosecute the intruder. The simpler "contain, clean, and deny access" may not provide evidence needed to identify and prosecute the criminal.

When the "contain, clean and deny access" approach is selected, an organization will use a range of techniques, such as denying access to "bad IP addresses," further restricting services using a firewall, or router to filter traffic, or just disconnecting the target system(s) from the network.

Both approaches have advantages and disadvantages. It is best to determine your policy in advance of a serious incident. Involve management in this decision, as ultimately the risk to the business environment belongs to them. Each system or application, based upon its business criticality, can have an incident handling approach assigned to it. It is ultimately up to top management to make the decision on which approach will be used, but this decision needs to be made prior to an incident and formalized in the incident handling procedures.

After you determine your organizational approach to incident handling, it will be much easier to determine under what conditions you are going to approach law enforcement.

Action 1.1.6 Establish automated intrusion detection

An intrusion detection system (IDS) can provide an early alerting mechanism when a system intrusion is in progress. Commercial products and freeware tools such as Snort (www.snort.org) can be set up to monitor critical network segments to watch for attacks. In addition, use host-based agents on critical servers to issue an alert when individual systems may be under attack. Prioritize alerts and tune the IDS to reduce "false positives" and produce quality alarms. If the incident should ever cause your organization to end up in court, an IDS can often serve as a second source of data to show that the logs on the system were not tampered with or fabricated.

NOTE: Some IDS products can be configured to automatically respond to an incident, for example, by terminating an attacker's connection or reconfiguring the firewall access control list. Caution should be employed when configuring an IDS in this manner because clever attackers will be able to use automatic response to trick your IDS into taking unwanted actions.

Action 1.1.7 Establish a policy for outside "peer" notification

A rapidly growing class of computer security incidents involves network-based denial-of-service attacks that spoof (impersonate) that is, address in such a way that a person outside your organization can cause your computers to attack another organization. Your organization should develop a policy stating whom to inform, when to inform, and how to inform outside organizations that your computing resources are being used to assault these outside agencies. It is good practice to be at least as responsive to incidents in which your organization is the source of the problem as you are when you are attacked. In these modern incidents, your organization can be made to appear to be the source of an attack when it is not. Write procedures that incorporate communication with the originating sites and the target sites.

Establish a policy for dealing with incidents involving remote computers belonging to you or to your employees and those involving contractors and other non full-time employees. As more employees routinely work at home or on the road, more security incidents will affect the remote systems or be initiated by remote systems. Establish a policy concerning search and seizure of such systems. Include consultants, temporary employees, and sub contractors. Be sure your organization's Acceptable Use Policies include home computers and portable computers. Establish a system through which you routinely record every outside person, such as a consultant, who is given access to systems and information. The records should detail the access that was granted. And as part of that policy, establish guidelines and mechanisms to remove their access when they cease employment, or are transferred or when access is no longer required. Where possible, make security guidelines mandatory in contracts with all outside vendors, contractors and consultants.

Action 1.1.8 Establish extranet (partnernet) agreements and monitoring

Establish agreements with all outside organizations connected to your network that give your organization the right to disconnect and monitor as needed. Some organizations prefer to use contract language that requires all parties to inform the others immediately if an incident occurs. Ensure that security requirements are included in service level agreements (SLAs) and are in alignment with already established SLAs.

Action 1.1.9 Identify critical assets and servers

Perform a risk assessment to identify your company's critical computing assets. Determine the impact that a system might have if it were to become unavailable or have confidential data exposed. One technique is to use is a numeric scale of likelihood (from 1 to 5) and cost of impact (from 1 to 5) where 1 is low risk/cost and 5 is high risk/cost.° Add the two together and you can rank your risks numerically by sorting high to low. Spend extra time protecting these systems and take additional steps to secure these systems such as encrypting sensitive data and using host-based intrusion detection. If possible the system's owners should be involved in determining the criticality.

FOR SMALL ORGANIZATIONS

How can a small organization afford to implement all of the suggestions in this booklet? Are there some core nuggets we can use?

Implement the most common recommendations. The most common advice from incident handlers who reviewed this document:

- Remain calm throughout the incident and take copious notes.
- Warning Banners: make sure you have them.
- Have employees, consultants, contractors, sign an acceptable use policy yearly.
- Ensure systems are properly secured before connecting them to the Internet and continuously after that.
- If connected to the Internet, ensure you have network monitoring: Snort is available at www.snort.org, TCPdump is available from www.tcpdump.org. Ethereal is available from www.ethereal.com/, versions of each of these tools can be used on Windows and Unix computers.
- Learn to use forensics tools in advance of the incident: the coroner's toolkit available at www.porcupine.org/forensics/tct.html, a favorite for technically advanced teams.
- Other free internet resources include those listed in the Resources Section at the end of this guide, which many handlers have found useful.
- Back up systems regularly.
- When recovering from backups, be careful not to reintroduce the vulnerability exploited by the attacker.
- Write a summary of what happened, what you did, and what you learned, so the lessons may be passed on.

Action 1.1.10 Use strong account policies

Idle accounts and accounts with weak passwords are incidents waiting to happen. Define and enforce strong password policies that include expiration, password complexity rules (such as upper and lowercase characters) and password history so that passwords are not reused. Tools like John the Ripper (www.openwall.com/john/) can be used to assess passwords. There are also tools for Unix and Windows to assess the strength of passwords as they are created.

Action 1.1.11 (Advanced) Perform a legal review of your policies and procedures

If your company intends (or may intend) to take legal action in the event of an incident, your policies and procedures should be reviewed by qualified legal professionals. This will prevent technicalities from undermining an otherwise strong legal case.

STEP 1.2 DEVELOP MANAGEMENT SUPPORT FOR AN INCIDENT HANDLING CAPABILITY

Problem: ***Until you have management buy-in, you'll find it hard to get time, money, and political support for your incident handling activities.***

Action 1.2.1 Create a formal, written security incident response plan

Creating a formal incident handling plan will ensure that everyone understands how security events will be handled. This plan should be regularly updated and should include common incident scenarios and their solutions, along with escalation paths and a contact list. A sample incident plan and an incident plan template are available at (www.sans.org/newlook/resources/policies).

Align your incident response plan with business needs. Keep relevant articles in a folder. Add printed copies of famous web server break-ins such as the one at the Department of Justice. The CIO Institute (www.cio.org) produced a particularly effective version of this story. It tells the story of Dr. Mark Boster, the Deputy Assistant Attorney General for Information Systems, who was responsible for the Justice Department systems that were attacked, and the nine lessons he and his team learned. One useful lesson was that he needed to increase the number of people assigned to monitor security.

Articles and booklets can help you get management's attention. Whenever you attend a meeting related to the incident handling team, carry the folder with you. Develop worst-case scenarios for intrusions into your business critical systems, which show the effect that it would have on the company monetarily and image-wise.

Action 1.2.2 Graphically illustrate an incident

Take the time to illustrate one or two of the incidents in your folder. Create a chart showing where the attackers came from, the vulnerabilities they used to get in, and what they were able to access. Help your organization's decision makers understand the consequences if the incident had not been detected. This action can empower your management because once they understand an incident, and can explain it to their peers, they become a proponent.

Action 1.2.3 Collect historical support

Keep executive summaries from previous incidents in the folder. Include information related to the cost of incidents. This should include damage to reputation, loss of productivity due to system downtime, and time spent on incident investigation. You should also consider money that was saved by rapid and professional response.

Action 1.2.4 Grant authority to the incident response team

Having the authority to make difficult decisions in the midst of a crisis can mean the difference between success and failure. Determine the level of authority you are granting the incident handling team to make critical decisions, including the authority to take servers offline and disconnect networks. Ensure that management supports and understands the level of authority the incident team will have in the event of a problem, and document this in your formal incident handling plan.

STEP 1.3 SELECT INCIDENT HANDLING TEAM MEMBERS AND ORGANIZE THE TEAM

***Problem:* Incident handling isn't a one-person job. Having the right people in the right place with the right preparation can make all the difference.**

Action 1.3.1 Identify qualified people to join the team

Write down the names that occur to you and their contact information. Talk to your co-workers and management about forming a local incident handling capability. Select a team that includes more than system administrators with security responsibilities. Include trained management and representatives from information security, risk management, human resources and the legal department to help make the hard decisions about whether to shut down core business systems in order to preserve your organization from even greater harm. Identify subject area experts and keep their contact information on file.

Action 1.3.2 Choose local, centralized, or combination teams

Your team will have two parts: a Command Decision Team to coordinate activities, and an On Site Incident Handling Team. In some cases these may be the same people; in others they are different.

The On Site Team goes to the location(s) of the incident. Team members secure the area, survey the situation and begin containment, eradication and recovery.

The Command Decision Team translates the technically oriented assessments of the On Site Team into the recovery steps that management directs the organization to take. They work with the organization's public affairs and legal staff if information needs to be provided to outside organizations or to the public. They are also responsible for keeping senior management advised of the status of the incident as appropriate.

Quick action requires that you decide, in advance, what organizations and functions will be represented on both of those teams. Start the planning process by considering what would happen if your organization needed to handle multiple concurrent incidents.

In a multiple-incident situation, the experienced handlers need to triage the situation and assign less trained personnel to some of the incidents. In such a situation, reliance on local support is often required. One corporation uses a staged response and responds from the corporate level o¸Æy if multiple corporate sites are being affected or if the incident involves a new type of attack. Alternatively, for organizations with multiple sites, the team could be drawn from representatives from each site. Very large organizations that try to handle all incidents with a core team at a single facility sometimes find that travel time lowers their ability to respond quickly.

Action 1.3.3 Identify the correct individuals in your organization's Public Affairs Office (PAO)

The PAO team is responsible for answering questions from the public regarding organizational activities. When a security-related incident occurs, it is also PAO's responsibility to disseminate appropriate information to the public. Your public affairs team may also be valuable support for incident handling. They usually have very good access to senior management and can help coordinate communications between the team and senior executives.

NOTE: Dealing directly with the press can be hazardous to your career. There is a huge risk of being misquoted, taken out of context, or of releasing information that is sensitive or even harmful to your organization. All press interaction should take place through the PAO with the help of management and the Incident Response team.

Action 1.3.4 Update your organization's disaster recovery plan to include computer incident handling

Certain critical business systems may have requirements for hot spare systems and/or back-up sites. Redundant machines and networks may allow you to take a compromised host down without impacting business processing. Ensure that your organization's disaster recovery plan includes 24-hour contact information with all key people. Test disaster recovery procedures regularly.

Action 1.3.5 Establish visibility and a compensation plan for the team

Incident handlers and the system administrators they count on for support often have to put in extraordinary effort in responding to an incident. Negotiate with management in advance, to provide mechanisms for recognition and compensation. Ensure that overtime will be paid and that time off can be granted to those who work long hours responding to security incidents.

Action 1.3.6 Provide checklists and network diagrams

Checklists for incident handling procedures help every member of the team to avoid errors and take the right steps toward incident resolution. In complex environments, diagrams and configuration documents should be provided that reflect network topology, including router ACLs and firewall rule sets. Make these documents part of your formal security incident handling plan.

STEP 1.4 DEVELOP AN EMERGENCY COMMUNICATIONS PLAN

***Problem:* Maintaining communications and keeping the right people informed are well understood, essential tasks. However, when facing new, unexpected events that are likely to occur during incidents, natural communication channels break down.**

Action 1.4.1 Create a call list and establish methods for informing people quickly

Use the communications form in the back of this guide to record as many contacts and phone numbers as you can. Establish a locator for all system administrators and have contact information of every system administrator and network person. Record work, cell, and home phone numbers for employees and alternate phone numbers where they may be likely to be found if not at home when an emergency occurs. Record pager numbers and, if the pager can be reached via the web or email, record relevant broadcast information. Many organizations send out a short message (such as 911) letting people know to call a voice mailbox where they place a full message detailing the status of the incident. This way, incident handling resources are not wasted repeating the same message as people are getting up to speed.

Action 1.4.2 Create an incident notification call tree

After an incident has been identified and the On Site Incident Handling Team has been dispatched to the location, a call tree can be used to contact many people in your organization. A call tree allows one call to a department in your organization to initiate calls to the rest of the key people in that department. You may already have such a tree as part of your organization's disaster recovery plan. If not, your organizational chart makes an excellent starting point. Test the call tree and call list at least once a year. **Note:** Direction to use the call tree should come from the Command Decision Team.

Action 1.4.3 Use offsite backup for call lists and call trees

Keep copies of the call list and call tree at an offsite location, and make sure the incident team members know the location of this information. In addition, experienced incident response professionals should carry contact information with them at all times.

Action 1.4.4 Ensure passwords and encryption keys are up-to-date and accessible

No matter how good your call lists are, some system administrators may not be available during a critical incident. Ensure that the passwords used to obtain root, superuser, or administrator access to every system and LAN within your organization are recorded on paper, and sealed in signed , small, well labeled envelopes, which are kept in a large sealed envelope. These should be signed across the seal so tampering is obvious, and secured in locked containers that can be accessed by the handling team. Usually, this is done at a local or department level. Establish procedures to ensure that these passwords stay current. The same process is useful for storing encryption keys for critical information. Make sure your procedures include provisions for verifying the identity of the person who needs a password or encryption key during an emergency. When access is no longer required, ensure that passwords are changed and the new keys are locked away.

Action 1.4.5 Establish a primary point of contact and an incident command and communications center

Effective coordination requires a single point of contact (POC). Otherwise no one knows who is in charge. For larger incidents, that person should be the leader of a Command Post Team that establishes a communication and response center. The center should be a place with plenty of phone lines, voice mailboxes, and fax machines. Some of these phone and fax lines should be outside lines, rather than lines routed through your organization's PBX. One reviewer, who worked on the response following the Northridge earthquake, suggests a portable generator, cellular phones, cellular modem jacks, and lots of spare batteries to supplement land lines. The facility should also have hard copies of all incident procedures and contact information.

Action 1.4.6 (In highly critical sites) Establish secured communications

In a major incident, it is possible that both the computer systems and the PBX might be penetrated. In fact, in a large number of incidents, the perpetrator is an employee or contractor of your organization and is well positioned to monitor your communications. In such a situation, encrypted telephones (including encrypted cell phones) and fax systems might be the only way the team can maintain communications without the attacker knowing their every move. Available tools include Pretty Good Privacy (PGP), secure web pages, and secure news groups for all team-to-team communications.

Action 1.4.7 Set up resource acquisition plans for the teams

Both teams should have procedures for ordering food, lodging, software, and other necessary resources for use during an incident. The On Site Team should maintain a response, or jump kit with backup software and hardware, boot diskettes for common operating systems, OS distribution media for common operating systems, blank floppies, and portable printers.

STEP 1.5 PROVIDE EASY REPORTING FACILITIES

Problem: ***When users do not know who to contact or what to say, they delay reporting information about possible security incidents. Most buildings have fire alarm systems that enable employees to report quickly and conveniently. Reporting computer security incidents should be nearly as easy as reporting a fire.***

Action 1.5.1 Educate users early

New employee briefings and orientation provide an ideal opportunity to inform employees about the organization's incident handling procedures and contact process. Memory fades over time, however, so you should not count on this initial briefing—your organization's incident response should be part of your yearly security awareness briefing.

Action 1.5.2 Publish a list of indicators of an incident

A list of indicators can assist your team and others in recognizing an incident when they see it. Examples of indicators to include: activity in previously idle accounts, unusual offsite access, new setuid root scripts, transfer of /etc/passwd in ftp and web logs, system crashes, unexplained filling of file systems, gaps in accounting logs, new or unfamiliar file names, and similar anomalies. Work with your system administrators to establish a list of indicators that are suited to the mix of operating systems that your organization uses. Let system administrators know that it is worth the extra effort to look into suspicious activity and report it as soon as possible.

Action 1.5.3 Use the web

Develop and maintain an Intranet Incident Web Page to help users locate your computer incident handling team. Each department should have a printed copy of this information in case the network or web server is unavailable during the incident. You can also use the web page to help keep your organization informed of changes.

Action 1.5.4 Encourage email and/or phone reporting

Establish a simple, easy-to-remember mail alias, such as incident@(yourorganization).org for users to report incidents. Several organizations have established toll free hotlines so users can report security incidents anonymously.

Action 1.5.5 Reward reporting

One organization recognizes employees who identify incidents or odd events with a NAATS Award (Not Asleep At the Switch). Another organization publishes the picture of alert employees with a short description of how they detected the incident and how their alertness aided the organization. Still another organization uses a cash reward as an incentive to encourage reporting.

Action 1.5.6 Continually update management

Keep management informed about threats, cost of incidents, security requirements, and similar information.

Action 1.5.7 Define incident parameters and requirements for incident escalation

Define the requirements that would need to be met before raising the alarm with senior management within your organization or to external law enforcement agencies such as the FBI. Make sure that any such contact has the approval of management and the PAO.

Action 1.5.8 Maintain reporting forms for incidents

Prepare forms, such as the ones included in this booklet, for recording incident information. Using prepared forms will ensure that incident notes are thorough enough to capture all required information.

STEP 1.6 CONDUCT TRAINING FOR TEAM MEMBERS

Problem: ***Untrained and under-prepared staff could be a disaster in the event of a real incident. Responding to an incident can put a lot of pressure on the incident team; a properly trained team will help make events flow smoothly.***

Action 1.6.1 Set up a planning/training meeting on scenarios

Plan and conduct a session for the incident handling team to discuss how to handle basic scenarios. Examples might include a virus epidemic, failed computer penetration attempt, successful computer penetration, or the discovery of a significant volume of child pornography on a corporate computer. Determine how these incidents would be handled. Decide whether resources outside the organization would need to be involved. Follow up the mock scenarios with the lessons learned process (see the Lessons Learned section and form for further information). Write the example scenarios and responses into your formal incident response plan.

Action 1.6.2 Set up tools and techniques training

Establish training for incident handling team members on using tools and techniques for backup, evidence collection, and analysis. Create a CD or floppy with forensics tools, including trusted command interpreters. (It is useful to ensure that the legal team review these tools in advance if you plan to use their output as evidence.) Ensure that team members are instructed to never execute programs directly on a compromised host. Ensure that the tools you have selected have been approved for forensic analysis and that they do not disrupt or alter evidence on the target system. It is a good idea to create a "jump bag" that contains everything you would need to respond to an incident at a moment's notice. This could include items ranging from forensic software to backup media to tape recorders, digital cameras and notepads.

Action 1.6.3 Stock some high capacity drives

Because backups are one of the most important activities you will undertake, be prepared by having high-capacity disks, their instruction manuals, and a variety of cables and terminators ready. Practice using them on a variety of hardware configurations before you need to use them under pressure.

Action 1.6.4 (Advanced) Conduct War Games

Run simulation sessions for system administrators and incident handling team members, where some of the members act as attackers and others as defenders. Don't restrict the war games to senior personnel; an entry-level system administrator is as likely to be involved in a large incident as a senior-level administrator. Update your incident response plan to reflect any issues that arise during live training. While simulations like the SANS IDNET provide the best results, paper practice scenarios are much cheaper and help keep your team sharp.

STEP 1.7 ESTABLISH GUIDELINES FOR INTER-DEPARTMENTAL COOPERATION

***Problem:* When an incident occurs, there is no shortage of people who want to help. If organizational roles and cooperation are not worked out in advance, some of the helpers may make the problem worse.**

Action 1.7.1 Encourage local handling of minor incidents

Users and local system administrators should be able to handle minor incidents such as virus infections. The organization's incident policy should define which incidents users and system administrators may handle by themselves and which they should report.

Action 1.7.2 Coordinate closely with help desks

The first indication of a problem may be a user reporting to a help desk. Help desks can be an excellent first line of defense for minor incidents such as virus infections affecting multiple machines. Many help desks have extended hour service even if they do not offer 24 x 7. Consider making the help desk part of the incident handling team and use them as your point of contact to report incidents.

Help desks are also a primary target for social engineering attacks. The classic attack is the phone call saying, "I have a very hot deadline to deliver the Frammitz reports to the V.P. of Operations and well, darn, I forgot my password. Could you please give me a new one?" If help desk staff are a part of your incident handling process, they will be aware of the types of attacks that are directed against your organization, and will be less likely to be vulnerable to social engineering. In addition, many organizations have help desk workers monitor network management and intrusion consoles anyway, so they are already trained in initial screening, reporting and, possibly, response to incidents. Finally, if the user of a system sees that he has a problem, but does not realize it is related to a compromise, he will probably report it to the help desk.

Action: Report and record. If a user suspects a serious incident, after reporting, policy should be to record what he has seen. The help desk may be the ideal place to file the report. In many organizations, the support engineer serves as a redundant communications channel, should automated alerts become compromised or fail in general. This can have an additional benefit to the organization since the help desk operator gains a sense of involvement and thus, will take a deeper and more proactive interest in the duties he or she is assigned.

STEP 1.8 PAY PARTICULAR ATTENTION TO RELATIONSHIPS WITH SYSTEM ADMINISTRATORS

Problem: ***The system administrator is the individual most often responsible for operational security for a subset of machines at a site or facility. They have their fingers on the pulse of the computer systems. Alert system administrators have detected many incidents by noticing some event that is strange, and by reviewing a system's log files. On the other hand, system administrators have the potential to do great harm in an incident. With privileged accounts they can alert intruders that they have been detected, destroy evidence or even destroy system files in a frantic attempt to eradicate an intruder.***

Action 1.8.1 Involve system administrators

Invite system administrators from different sections to consult in the incident handling process. A fresh set of eyes brings the perspective needed to solve problems in the most efficient manner.

Action 1.8.2 Conduct proactive training

Offer workshops for system administrators on available software packages to help detect attacks and accomplish effective system monitoring. The most effective instructors are usually people who can relate first-hand experience in handling incidents and in using the tools. Plan to require GIAC security certification for system and network administrators.

Action 1.8.3 Recognize "power" log file reading

The indicators of many never-detected incidents are buried in log files. It is not enough to collect system logs; it is important to also read them. Obtain tools to facilitate log file analysis and to automate the process as much as possible. Ensure that your log retention policy is sufficient to support in-depth investigations, where logs from weeks or months prior might be required. System administrators who detect incidents should be recognized and rewarded.

Action 1.8.4 Encourage regular system backups

Inadequate backups have been the cause of many catastrophes in recovering from security incidents. Up-to-date, clean, bombproof, or offsite backups are essential. Strongly encourage system administrators to keep their backups current and to verify that their tape drives are working correctly by testing the backups. In order to encourage backups of system that may have fallen through the cracks, one organization sends a note to all employees during the first week of December suggesting that if they haven't ensured their systems were backed up that year, now might be a good time. Critical systems should be backed up at least daily. Ensure that offsite backups can be retrieved in a timely manner. Every incident handling team member should be familiar with the organization's commercial backup software as well as with free tools like "dd" for Unix systems and "ntbackup" for Windows systems.

Action 1.8.5 Ensure that auditing and logging are enabled and sufficient

Make sure that sufficient auditing and logging are turned on before an incident takes place. In addition, make sure that system clocks are synchronized from a trusted time source. This will ensure that log files accurately reflect the real time that an incident took place. When possible send logs to duplicate log servers. For instance, with the syslog facility, it is a simple matter to keep a local log and send a duplicate copy to a syslog server.

Action 1.8.6 Ensure that systems run antivirus software with current definitions

Antivirus software can help protect a system not only from viruses, Trojan horses, worms, and other malicious code. Antivirus software is only effective when definitions are updated regularly. Most sites update daily, as Jimmy Kuo, a senior researcher at NAI would say, "you are only as good as your last update". Make sure that you can easily distribute antivirus updates in the event of an outbreak. Antivirus software should be present on every computing resource in your enterprise, including desktops, servers, and email gateways. It is a good idea to check from time to time to make sure it is actually running; modern malicious code will attempt to terminate antivirus and personal firewall programs. It may be advisable to run more than one brand of antivirus scanner at your email gateways as these will be at the point of a large number of attacks.

Action 1.8.7 Be familiar with server configurations and operating systems

You should be familiar with common operating system processes like lsass.exe on Windows NT/2000 and syslogd on UNIX. For Internet facing systems, document the processes that should be running on the systems. If you are able to recognize ordinary system processes, you will also be able to quickly spot programs that are unusual. These programs could be Trojans or backdoors placed on your system by attackers. Run cryptographic hashing algorithms like MD5 or SHA-1 or install software like Tripwire to monitor the integrity of critical system files.

Action 1.8.8 Perform penetration testing

One of the best ways to prevent incidents is to ensure that your systems are not vulnerable in the first place. Conduct regular penetration tests to make sure that your systems are configured securely and that system patches have been applied. One approach is to do the testing in three stages: 1) "War-Dialing" to discover unauthorized modems and poorly-configured authorized ones; 2) external testing to see what an "outsider" can discover and exploit about your system; and 3) internal testing to see what an "insider" can discover and exploit about your system. Many sites prefer this approach to a "capture the flag" wargames style test. If you do not have the resources for true penetration testing, at least run a vulnerability scanner like nessus.

STEP 1.9 DEVELOP INTERFACES TO LAW ENFORCEMENT AGENCIES AND OTHER COMPUTER INCIDENT RESPONSE TEAMS (CIRTS)

***Problem:* When you need help in a hurry, you'll get it far more easily if you have established relationships in advance. Multiple law enforcement agencies may have overlapping responsibilities for computer incident handling. The challenge is determining how to find and contact the people who are knowledgeable about computer incidents.**

Action 1.9.1 Familiarize yourself with applicable laws

Familiarize yourself with the local, state, and federal laws regarding computer crime, including the rules of handling evidence and of criminal prosecution. If your intention is to prosecute (and even if it is not), you should understand concepts like chain of custody and what constitutes legally admissible evidence.

Action 1.9.2 Know the types of cases law enforcement will be interested in

Law enforcement is primarily concerned with apprehending and prosecuting criminals. Law enforcement agencies care about the following areas: computer trespasses, theft, espionage, child pornography, hate crimes, threats, and stalking. On the other hand, these agencies may not be able to assist in the response. They may provide no more than a cursory investigation if the evidence has not been preserved, or if the case does not appear to be worth the investment in prosecution (e.g., because the incident is extremely minor or the economic damage associated with it is too low).

Action 1.9.3 Contact local law enforcement before there is an incident

Now is the time to get to know your local law enforcement computer crime officers. They are often willing to provide computer crime awareness education to your organization and to meet with your management. They can also help you determine local, state, and national requirements for handling evidence. Get all the contact information you can: phone numbers, pager numbers, e-mail addresses, and so forth. Include law enforcement contact information in your organization's site-specific incident handling guidelines. Relationships of any sort are an investment; in an incident these people could prove to be your organization's best friends. Some sites strongly recommend that a single person be named as the law-enforcement liaison.

Action 1.9.4 Join or create a CIRT or FIRST team

If a Computer Incident Response Team, or coordinating entity for organizations like yours exists, get to know the members and establish mechanisms for getting help when you need it. InfraGard, a program run by the NIPC, is popular in the United States. More information is available at: www.InfraGard.net. If you use PGP, include your CIRT's public key on your key ring.

PHASE 2. IDENTIFICATION

Identification involves determining whether or not an incident has occurred, and, if one has occurred, determining the nature of the incident. Identification normally begins after someone has noticed an anomaly in a system or network. This phase also includes informing and soliciting help from the people who can help you understand and solve the problem. It is important to recognize at this point that not every network or system anomaly will be a security incident. Too often, people leap to the conclusion that there's a hostile intent behind every problem.

A FEW WORDS ON PHASES 2-6

Nearly half of this guide was used to outline Phase I, the Preparation Phase. This makes sense because an organization that is well prepared is in position to act quickly and effectively when a computer security incident occurs. The remaining steps are divided into five additional phases that are put into practice when an incident occurs: Identification (Phase 2), Containment (Phase 3), Eradication (Phase 4), Recovery (Phase 5), and Lessons Learned (Phase 6).

STEP 2.1 ASSIGN A PERSON TO BE RESPONSIBLE FOR THE INCIDENT

Problem:* *Without a central point of control, too many people may be working at cross-purposes. Undirected activities could cause the misdiagnosis of the nature of the incident, loss of forensic evidence, and possibly creation of a worse situation than the incident by itself would have caused.

Action 2.1.1 Select a person to handle or coordinate identification and assessment

If at all possible, the method for selecting a person as an incident handler should be predefined. This person should have broad general knowledge of the enterprise, and have some experience in handling incidents and problem determination. If the Command Decision Team and On Site Team are in different locations, it is imperative the two teams remain in communication using secure means throughout the incident. Because incidents often take place during off-hours, weekends or holidays, a pool of several potential handlers should be identified and be familiar with the security policies and procedures. And they should know where to find the contact and escalation lists developed during the preparation phase, both internal and external.

Action 2.1.2 Begin a log of the incident

From the very beginning of a suspected incident, the person handling the incident should start taking notes on each step, identifying who did what, when and how and why they did it. The notes should be chronological, with the time of each entry indicated. Keep the log as factual as possible; care should be taken to avoid speculation. Avoid statements like "The hacker has clearly erased the system logs"; instead use a statement like "The system logs do not show any entries for a period of six hours." Log entries must be statements of fact; careless speculation can confuse the evaluation of the incident, and when repeated in court, could damage a legal case.

STEP 2.2 DETERMINE WHETHER OR NOT AN EVENT IS ACTUALLY AN INCIDENT

Problem: ***Evidence indicating a potential security incident often turns out to indicate something less. If a situation is misdiagnosed, it is often easy to make the data "fit" the misdiagnosis. An analogy is that anyone can pull the red handle if they think there is a fire, but only the fire team can make the determination that a seven-alarm fire has broken out or that the problem has been contained and no further action is necessary.***

Action 2.2.1 Check for simple mistakes

Examples of simple mistakes include errors in system configuration or an application program, hardware failures, and, most commonly, user or system administrator errors. A seasoned incident handling professional, who has seen many cases, can often make the determination with just a few questions of the local system administration staff. Taking the time to evaluate the configurations for simple mistakes has a dual purpose: it is also possible to expose other related problems or vulnerabilities through this initial examination process. Once the simple mistakes have been quantified or ruled out, it is much easier to determine the total scope of the incident.

Action 2.2.2 Assess the evidence in detail

Use the list of indicators you developed during the preparation phase to quickly assess the possible type of incident.

STEP 2.3 BE CAREFUL TO MAINTAIN A PROVABLE CHAIN OF CUSTODY

Problem: ***The events that you see and the evidence you collect may be excellent, but they won't be worth much in a courtroom unless you can prove six months later that these are the exact events that happened, and are the same evidence you collected during the incident. Maintaining a clear chain of evidence may become critical in the event that the incident ends up in a legal case. The opposition will challenge each item. If they can show that someone has had the opportunity to modify the evidence during or after the time it was collected, they can radically reduce the legal impact of the evidence.***

Action 2.3.1 Identify every piece of evidence

Unless you are facing a dire emergency where you must immediately unplug the system to stop damage, before you touch the computer, begin to identify the evidence. Your logs should state the day and time, and describe your location and any serial numbers or other identifying information. Law enforcement agencies may request that suspect disk drives be removed and sealed as evidence. If they have identifying information—make, model or serial number—be certain to record that. In addition, plans should be in place to recover both hardware and backup data. Even older backup tapes that predate the incident may provide valuable evidence. Whenever copies of electronic data are made, the original data, not the copy, should then be sealed for evidence.

Number, date, and sign notes and printouts. Seal disks with original, unaltered, complete logs in an envelope or other container; then number, date, and sign the container. When you turn evidence over to the appropriate person in your organization, have the recipient sign for each item. If evidence is turned over to law enforcement, ensure every item turned over is detailed and signed for as part of your chain of custody process. Original handwritten notes should be copied, and the original notes sealed as part of the chain of custody. Electronic data should be captured as soon as possible, and the process of making copies of the evidence should be witnessed.

Action 2.3.2 Control access to evidence

Identify an evidence custodian to ensure that you can prove who has access to the secure container used to store the evidence – and this is a very small group of people. If there is a key lock, each key should be stamped *do not duplicate*. Make sure, by policy and practice, that each person with access understands they are required to control access to these items. Any and every person with access to the evidence may have to testify if the incident results in a court trial.

STEP 2.4 COORDINATE WITH THE PEOPLE WHO PROVIDE YOUR NETWORK SERVICES

***Problem:* Many of the corrective actions may require the assistance of your ISP. Filters may need to be applied, or routing tables modified before the network traffic reaches your site. In addition there may be forensic evidence in the ISP's logs that should be protected.**

Action 2.4.1 Coordinate closely with your Internet Service Provider

Inform your ISP of your initial evidence or opinion, and ask the ISP to assist in the investigation. If possible, it is helpful to have contact names and numbers of the senior personnel at the ISP prior to the incident. Many hours can be lost navigating through the average help desk escalation procedures. You need to reach those people who have the capacity and experience to evaluate the logs and to make changes to the network equipment.

To protect themselves against user complaints, most ISPs will ask for a properly executed court order before sharing any information they gather with you. Unfortunately normal log rotation schedules may destroy evidence before a court order can be obtained. To protect the data, ask your ISP to set aside copies of their logs as a courtesy until a final determination is made about whether a court order is merited.

STEP 2.5 NOTIFY APPROPRIATE OFFICIALS

***Problem:* Computer incidents, fires, and medical emergencies are usually a lot easier to handle when reported promptly. If you saw a co-worker in the cafeteria collapse, hopefully you wouldn't wait until the next day to alert the emergency medical system.**

Action 2.5.1 Notify your local or organizational incident handling team

Notify your manager and security officer as soon as the incident is suspected. It is far too easy to begin working through an incident and forget to involve the management team. It is the responsibility of the management team to insure that proper notifications are made and that the necessary resources are made available to the team. It is a common practice to have the incident handler separate from the designated contact for management, so that the handler is able to focus on coordinating the technical activities. A management person should work closely with the handler in order to keep the management chain of command informed and involved.

PHASE 3. CONTAINMENT

The goal of the containment phase is to limit the scope and magnitude of an incident—to keep the incident from getting worse.

STEP 3.1 DEPLOY THE ON-SITE TEAM TO SURVEY THE SITUATION

Problem: ***If data is not gathered quickly and accurately, it may never be gathered.***

Action 3.1.1 Deploy a small team

Four or five people are the limit for an On site Team at one location. The risk of loss of coordination leading to errors and the overhead of incident communication goes up with a larger team. Also, if this incident should ever go to court, everyone who stays in the area is a potential witness.

Action 3.1.2 Secure the area using physical security personnel if possible.

Action 3.1.3 Use the survey forms provided in this guide, or from **www.sans.org/incidentforms**.

The fields in the survey forms will help ensure that all needed information is recorded.

Action 3.1.4 Review the information that was provided to you from the identification phase

Be very careful to check any conclusions others have reached.

Action 3.1.5 Keep the system(s) pristine

Do not allow the system to be altered in any way until the backup has been completed.

STEP 3.2 KEEP A LOW PROFILE

Problem: ***If a network-based intrusion is determined, be careful not to give away what you know.***

Action 3.2.1 Avoid using obvious methods to look for the intruder

A classic rookie error is to ping, nslookup, finger, telnet to, or in some other way make contact with the suspected source of the attack (hours later). If your adversaries detect you trying to locate them, they may delete your file systems and break off the connection (for a while anyway) in an effort to cover their tracks.

Action 3.2.2 Maintain standard procedures

If your site is protected by an active intrusion detection system that drops connections or blocks attacking IP addresses, do not disable the IDS to try to gather more data. This would create a change in your profile that might warn the attacker.

STEP 3.3 AVOID, IF POSSIBLE, POTENTIALLY COMPROMISED CODE

Problem: ***Intruders may install Trojan horses and similar malicious code in system binaries.***

Action 3.3.1 Be wary of compromised system binaries

It is not advisable to log in to a system suspected of being compromised, as "root" or "administrator," and then start typing commands such as ftp to download tools from another site. If possible, record the cryptographic fingerprint of critical binary files for the organization's core operating systems. Some experienced incident handlers recommend building disks with core binaries. In any case, the only binary you want to be particularly concerned about at this moment in an incident is the system's backup program.

STEP 3.4 BACKUP THE SYSTEM

Problem: ***Perpetrators of computer crime are becoming increasingly proficient in destroying evidence of illegal activity to avoid detection or prosecution. Therefore, it is extremely important to obtain a full backup, preferably using disk imaging of the system with known good binaries in which suspicious events have been observed.***

Action 3.4.1 Backup to new (unused) media

Do your backup as soon as there are indications that a security-related incident has occurred. Use new media because juries may be convinced that the "evidence is faulty" if it is written over old information. Making a full backup immediately captures evidence that otherwise may be destroyed before you and others have a chance to look at it. If possible, make two backups, one to keep sealed as evidence, and one to use as a source of additional backups. The backup will also provide a basis for comparison later in case you need to determine if any additional unauthorized activity has occurred. Disk-to-disk backup is often the fastest method. Though there are tools for some Unix systems that do destructive formats, in general if you have to reuse media you should not count on format to erase all of the previous data.

There are tools that clear disk by overwrite to U.S. Government standards such as BC Wipe. Finally, you could always try using dd, e.g. dd if=/dev/zero of=/dev/hdb.

Action 3.4.2 Safely store any backup tapes so that they will not be lost and/or stolen

Tape protection is an important part of the chain of custody of critical information. If tapes are unprotected, the entire case could be damaged.

STEP 3.5 DETERMINE THE RISK OF CONTINUING OPERATIONS

***Problem:* One of the most difficult decisions, and one subject to extreme pressure by end-users and senior management, is what to do about the compromised system. Here you will decide whether a system should be shut down entirely, disconnected from the network, or be allowed to continue to run in its normal operational status so that any activity on the system can be monitored.**

Action 3.5.1 Acquire logs and other sources of information

Many log files turn over fairly quickly, so it is important to acquire network and computer logs immediately.

Action 3.5.2 Review logs from neighboring systems

Review logs and cryptographic file signature databases from other systems on the same subnet and from systems that regularly connect to the affected system(s), especially if there is a trust relationship.

Lance Spitzner, founder of the Honeynet forensics project, tells a story we can all learn from. He had a system that he had used as a honeypot. It was put out on the Internet and compromised. He sent the code to be evaluated by the Honeynet forensics team. They sent it right back to him. The box had started out life as a Windows 98 system, then upgraded to NT and finally to Linux. There were artifacts of all these "lives" of previous systems on the disk, making forensics nearly impossible. We should learn two things from this: first, wipe and format drives, don't just upgrade, and second, there is a lot of data that is not part of the current operating system load on the disk. Only a binary backup will pick up this metadata.

Action 3.5.3 Make a recommendation

The On Site Team provides a recommendation to the Command Post Team, who will make the decision on what to do.

STEP 3.6 CONTINUE TO CONSULT WITH SYSTEM OWNERS

***Problem:* System owners' stress levels can be very high because their business may stop during the review process, and very large amounts of money may be lost.**

Action 3.6.1 Keep system owners and administrators briefed on progress

The users of the affected system almost invariably really need the system, usually for an important project due that day. There is also a tendency for the system administrator or manager responsible for the system to internalize the incident. They might become defensive because they sometimes feel that since they operate the affected computer, the situation is their fault. Keeping them informed and aware of progress can help lower the stress level.

Action 3.6.2 Never allow fault to be an issue during incident handling

As you work to contain an incident, try to take time to give your co-workers a smile, a pat on the back, and mention the things that are being done right as much as possible.

STEP 3.7 CHANGE PASSWORDS

***Problem:* A common target of intruders is root or administrator account names and passwords.**

Action 3.7.1 Change the password on the affected systems

In the case of system compromise, passwords should be changed on the compromised system and all systems it regularly interacts with.

Action 3.7.2 If a sniffer is detected or suspected, expand the password change order

If you have reason to believe your systems have been subjected to a sniffer attack, passwords may have been compromised on all systems on the affected LAN or subnet. If a large system such as a POP mail server is compromised, and the organization wants to keep rumors and questions to a minimum, it may be advisable to explain the password change as part of a system upgrade or as the routine recommendation of an external security auditor. Emphasize how important it is for users to change to a unique password that is not being used on any other computer system.

PHASE 4. ERADICATION

The goal of the eradication phase is to eliminate or mitigate the factor(s) that resulted in a compromise of system security. Compromise of a system can be traumatic for a system owner. But if the incident handling team fails to adequately eradicate the problem, and if another compromise occurs, then management can legitimately question the competency of the incident handling team itself.

STEP 4.1 DETERMINE CAUSE AND SYMPTOMS OF THE INCIDENT

Problem:* *You cannot fix the security problem that led to a system compromise if you don't know what happened.

Action 4.1.1 Isolate the attack and determine how it was executed

Information collected during the survey phase may be sufficient to determine the root cause of the incident. In most incidents, there are multiple causes for a compromise. The absence of adequate technical controls, for example, may result from the failure to adequately select and train system administrators; from the lack of written security policies and procedures; from the absence of management emphasis; or all of these reasons. Team members must conduct a comprehensive review of the data gathered, and not assume that one factor alone contributed to the compromise.

If for whatever reason, there is insufficient evidence to arrive at an exact understanding of the attack and how the attacker exploited a weakness, then team members may list all realistic possibilities based upon available information. From what is possible, the team can collectively develop scenarios to explain what has occurred. It may even be feasible to recreate the symptoms and to attempt an actual replication of the incident for additional forensic analysis using tools like the Honeynet (www.honeynet.org) or Coroner's Toolkit (www.porcupine.org/forensics/tct.html.)

STEP 4.2 IMPROVE DEFENSES

Problem:* *Once a system has been compromised, its password file, IP address, and operating system may get advertised to the hacker community. As a result, for weeks following the incident, the system may get repeatedly probed or attacked. New attackers may have enough data to launch attacks. More importantly, the original attacker may be unaware that the system's owner has discovered the compromise. That attacker may continue to return to the compromised system to obtain additional information and to use the compromised system as a springboard for attacks on other systems.

Action 4.2.1 Implement appropriate protection techniques such as firewall and/or router filters, moving the system to a new name/IP address, or in extreme cases, porting the machine's function to a more secure operating system.

The incident handling team cannot permit a compromised host to reestablish network connections until the team fully understands the cause(s) of the incident, and can direct the system's owner to follow specific eradication procedures that will preclude a re-occurrence. The team must always verify the correct implementation of those procedures before reconnection.

Depending on the environmental and operational factors involved, many procedures may be outside the control of the system's owner. For example, typically in large enterprises, firewall and router configurations are the responsibility of another organizational entity. The team should serve as the liaison between the system's owner and these entities to ensure adequate protection. Similarly, the system's owner may lack the technical expertise to re-build a system after a compromise. The incident handling team may have to provide assistance, or again serve as a liaison. Finally, the team may decide that the cause of the compromise was an insecure operating system or network environment that cannot be addressed by simply re-building an existing system or network. The team may then recommend that management approve a redeployment on a safer operating system before reconnection.

STEP 4.3 PERFORM VULNERABILITY ANALYSIS

***Problem:* Though prudence dictates that all sites that care about security perform regular vulnerability analyses of their systems and networks, many do not. When they experience a security incident, however, they usually act quickly to look for additional vulnerability analyses. The use of automated vulnerability assessment tools can assist an incident handling team not only to validate the correctness of eradication procedures, but also to anticipate and correct factors that might facilitate an attack.**

Action 4.3.1 Perform system vulnerability analysis

Use a system vulnerability tool to determine whether configuration and software versions at your site need to be updated. Either acquire a vulnerability analysis tool or hire a security consultant who brings one along.

Both host-based and network-based assessment tools can determine the robustness of system and network configurations. Host-based tools provide a higher degree of accuracy than do network-based tools. Increasingly host-based tools such as bastille, available at www.bastille-linux.org or the tools from the Center for Internet Security www.cisecurity.org/ have the capability to actually correct or to strengthen the security of a system. Network-based tools such as nmap, available at www.insecure.org/nmap or nessus, available at www.nessus.org can identify, and in some cases stress, common vulnerability exposures that may have resulted in a compromise. A combination of tools is beneficial because each tool may have unique capabilities.

Action 4.3.2 Search for related vulnerabilities

One critical step, often forgotten in the eradication phase, is to ensure other platforms within the organization are not vulnerable to the factor(s) that allowed the compromise. Incident handling team members can quickly use automated assessment tools to search for these factors. Team members must be aware, however, of two pieces of information that can facilitate the search. First, does the organization have an inventory of computing resources? If so, that inventory will expedite the search. Team members must recognize that, if they employ a network-based assessment tool, they may have no assurance that all potentially vulnerable systems are on-line at the time of search. Without a valid inventory of computing resources, any network search may be an exercise in hit-and-miss.

Second, does the organization have an effective configuration management program? If so, is the program centralized or decentralized? Inventories and centralized configuration capabilities will allow the team to focus its attention and resources productively when searching out and correcting related vulnerabilities.

STEP 4.4 REMOVE THE CAUSE OF THE INCIDENT

Problem: ***Deciding what to do to remove the cause is often a great challenge. The actions below provide high-level guidance. Additional guidance for each of the common types of attack is offered in a later section entitled "Special Actions for Responding to Various Types of Incidents".***

Action 4.4.1 For virus infestations

In the case of a virus, eradication simply requires removing the virus from all systems and media (e.g., floppy disks), usually with virus eradication software.

Action 4.4.2 For other malicious code infestations

Commercial software may exist to eradicate common or "in the wild" malicious code. Most commercial programs will identify computer viruses, well-known Trojan horses, and certain worms—all forms of malicious software for the Windows and Macintosh environments. For Unix environments there are few commercial programs available. However in most cases, dedicated professionals have released detection and removal tools into the public domain to address the influx of Trojan horses and worms that have appeared in UNIX systems within the last three years. The incident handling team must stockpile both commercial and free detection/eradication software in anticipation of an infection.

The team must recognize the potential for reinfection, given that it may be difficult to disinfect all media—particularly backup media. If backups become infected, then the potential for reinfection increases.

Finally, the team must ensure that there is an effective procedure by which updates to commercial anti-viral programs are available.

Action 4.4.3 For network intrusion

In the case of a network intrusion, eradication is more difficult. Many attacks over a network are in two parts. First there is an initial phase, where a system vulnerability is exploited and the system is accessed. Once in, the intruder often installs a tool (back door) to provide continued access. The intruder may also set up shop on the compromised system to use it for intrusions into other computers. There are many examples in which intruders have launched exploit scripts against other computers from a single compromised system. Attackers also often install backdoor access programs and sniffers to collect additional passwords and user ID's. Your team's job—often its most difficult job—is to search for all such programs and remove them.

The team must determine whether the attacker has modified the compromised system in any way (i.e., alterations of system binaries and files, installation of attack programs, creation of "backdoors" into the compromised system). The only practical way to do this is to immediately disconnect the compromised system from the network until such time as team members have completed forensic analysis. This assumes that team members have information as to what was the baseline "norm" of the system before compromise; and that they have access to clean, uncompromised system binaries and application programs installed on the compromised system.

If there are business reasons that preclude disconnection, then the team can consider alternatives. For example, it may be possible to place a firewall directly in front of the compromised system and establish an Access Control List (ACL) to preclude an attacker's access. Another possibility may be to filter incoming and possibly outgoing connections to and from the compromised system at the organization's network perimeter.

Finally, if law enforcement considerations dictate that monitoring the attacker takes precedence over eradication, then the system may be left in place with appropriate sensors to capture the attacker's keystrokes. Only senior management, not the incident handling team, or the legal department, has the right to approve such a course of action.

Action 4.4.4 If the attacker discovers your efforts

Sometimes the attackers will detect your eradication efforts and attempt to maintain control of your system. This is a tough situation for which you may wish to request law enforcement support. Continue in your efforts to remove the attacker's code from your system. Do everything possible to get network/phone logs of the attack. If the source address of the network traffic is not spoofed and if your policy allows, contact that owner for the source network and try to get their logs as well.

In some cases, attackers have actually contacted organizational personnel with offers to help in the eradication.

Each organization must have written policies and procedures in place to address such situations. The policy must indicate at what point the organization will report to and seek assistance from law enforcement agencies. Most importantly, the policy must identify who within the organization will make the decision, and who will make the contact.

Team members should refrain from direct contact with an attacker in the absence of written policy. If such contact does occur, team members must maintain detailed audit records of all contact. Once law enforcement personnel have responded to an incident, they—not organizational personnel—will usually manage all contacts. For this reason organizations should make liaison with respective law enforcement agencies in advance of an actual intrusion.

STEP 4.5 LOCATE THE MOST RECENT CLEAN BACKUP

***Problem:* In the next phase you'll restore the system to operation. First, however, you must locate a backup that is not infected and that is current.**

Action 4.5.1 Search for a current backup (i.e., pre-infestation or intrusion)

It can be hard to know just when the attack occurred, and this makes selecting your backup problematic. During the Code Red worm attack, the second version, "variant c" installed a back door onto the Windows NT or 2000 system running IIS. Most of the people affected by Code Red were unable to determine when their system was first compromised. Though there were tools to remove the infection, there was no way to know what had been done to the system while it was compromised. They had to choose between rebuilding the entire system from original media or restoring files from a backup created before the second version of Code Red was first detected in June 2001. In either case, high quality backups were critical.

In case of a root kit-style attack

A root kit attack embeds so much malicious code in so many hidden places in a computer system that cleaning the system is almost never a viable option. If there is evidence of a root kit style attack, it may be better to avoid the backups, nuke the disk, rebuild the operating system (without the vulnerability), configure the operating system safely, patch the operating system with the latest patches, and reload the data.

PHASE 5. RECOVERY

In the Recovery Phase, your task is to return the system to fully operational status.

STEP 5.1 RESTORE THE SYSTEM

Problem:* *Speed is critical, but a misstep at this stage may allow the attacker to re-enter the system later.

Action 5.1.1 Restore from backups or reload the entire system

Some incidents, such as malicious code, may require a complete restoration of operation from backups. In this case, it is essential to first determine the integrity of the backup itself. In general, the idea is to restore from the most recent backup made before the system was compromised. Make every effort to ensure that you are not restoring compromised code. If no backups have been made prior to compromise, you may have to rebuild the system from CD-ROM or other trusted media and apply patches, or to obtain and use a backup from a similar system that has not been compromised.

STEP 5.2 VALIDATE THE SYSTEM

Problem:* *Management and users want to know whether the problem has actually been eradicated.

Action 5.2.1 Once the system has been restored, verify that the operation was successful and the system is back to its normal condition.

Ideally there is a system test plan to evaluate the system. More commonly, the system is run through its normal tasks while being closely monitored by a combination of techniques such as network loggers and system log files. A caveat: sometimes patches or techniques used to prevent a vulnerability, will cause the system to function differently than it did before the event.

STEP 5.3 DECIDE WHEN TO RESTORE OPERATIONS

Problem:* *Uncertainty about whether all malicious code has been removed can cause long delays.

Action 5.3.1 Put the final decision in the hands of the system owners.

We suggest that the management of an affected system and their system administrators make these decisions. Quite often, they will be sufficiently sensitive to security threats that they may wish to leave the system offline for a couple days to do an operating system upgrade or even to install additional patches.

STEP 5.4 MONITOR THE SYSTEMS

Problem:* *Back doors and other malicious code can be very well hidden.

Action 5.4.1 Once the system is back on line, continue to monitor for back doors that escaped detection.

PHASE 6. FOLLOW-UP

In Phase 6, the goal is to learn from the incident. You are searching for lessons that will help you do a better job in the future. Some incidents require considerable time and effort. Stress levels rise and relationships may become strained. Afterwards, the folks who were at the center of the storm tend to want to forget it and get on with their lives. Performing follow-up activity, however, is one of the most valuable activities in responding to incidents. This procedure, only slightly more popular than wisdom tooth removal, is known as "the search for lessons learned". Organizations that follow up soon after problems have been contained find they rapidly improve their incident handling capability. Rapid follow up also helps support efforts to prosecute those who have broken the law.

STEP 6.1 DEVELOP A FOLLOW-UP REPORT

Problem:* *Experience must be captured quickly. A Follow-up report, including lessons learned, is the accepted method of protecting the knowledge so it can be used in the future.

Action 6.1.1 Start as soon as possible.

Folks who wait until weeks after the dust has settled, learn that the human memory, unlike fine wine, does not improve with the passage of time.

Action 6.1.2 Assign the task to the on site team.

In order to make the lessons learned section as positive and effective as possible, most sites require the incident handling team to draft the Lessons Learned Report as an integral part of their handling of the incident. The job's not finished until the paperwork is done.

Action 6.1.3 Include forms from this guide.

The incident report is generally an electronic version of the identification, survey, containment, and eradication forms that are included in this guide. Focus especially on answering the questions on the Lessons Learned form.

Action 6.1.4 Encourage all affected parties to review the draft.

Submit the Lessons Learned, along with the draft incident report, for review by all affected parties.

Action 6.1.5 Attempt to reach consensus.

Gather responses, disagreements, additions, and suggestions from all the interested parties. Encourage them to submit comments electronically, so they will do it quickly. Keep their comments as part of the record.

Action 6.1.6 Conduct a Lessons Learned meeting.

Distribute the comments in advance and plan for a one-hour Lessons Learned meeting. If you surprise people with comments they had not previously reviewed, meetings can take much longer. Focus the meeting on recounting the incident and ratifying any process changes.

Action 6.1.7 Create an Executive Summary.

Summarize the incident, including cost and impacts, for management. Submit the summary to management with a promise that recommended changes will follow.

Action 6.1.8 Send recommended changes to management.

Provide management with a prioritized set of recommended changes from the Lessons Learned process along with cost estimate, high-level schedule, and impact of implementing or not implementing the recommended actions.

Action 6.1.9 Implement approved actions.

Where you get management approval, ensure the changes are made using your organization's tasking system.

SPECIAL ACTIONS FOR RESPONDING TO VARIOUS TYPES OF INCIDENTS

In the previous sections we outlined actions that are applicable to a wide variety of computer security incidents. In this section, we define common types of incidents and suggest specific actions appropriate for dealing with each type.

TYPE 1. MALICIOUS CODE ATTACKS

Malicious code is the name given to programs such as viruses, Trojan horses, worms, and scripts used by crackers/hackers to gain privileges, capture passwords, and to modify audit logs to hide unauthorized activity. Malicious code is usually designed to be difficult to detect and trace. Certain viruses can even modify their signature. NOTE: Even when your firewalls and other defenses stop adversaries, those attackers may be able to accomplish the same objective with Trojan horse code pre-installed on computers you purchase. In general, you should not rely on a single security component, such as a firewall, or a virus checker, to reliably protect yourself against malicious code.

Special Action 1.1 Use virus checkers

Anti-virus software can be effective at preventing the spread of common viruses, Trojan horses, and worms. Ensure that anti-virus software is widely available and that the signature files are kept up to date. Consider employing mechanisms that automate signature updates.

Special Action 1.2 Encourage users to report suspicious activity

Encourage users to report suspicious activity to help you detect an infection early on; educated users can act as effective anomaly sensors. Unexplained disk activity, unusual system messages, strange processes, and unexplained software behavior could be a sign of malicious code infection. Advertise an e-mail address or a phone number where internal users can report suspicious activity.

Special Action 1.3 Monitor for abnormal outgoing traffic (Advanced)

Malicious code specimens may attempt to communicate with external systems through HTTP, IRC, and other outbound protocols to propagate, announce their location, or download updates. Focus network monitoring systems to detect inexplicable packets originating from your organization bound for the Internet. Such activity occurs most frequently at system boot up, especially at the first bootup after the initial infection.

Special Action 1.4 Protect the software load process by doing it yourself (Advanced)

Develop processes to install all operating system software and applications locally, from tested configurations. Discourage users from installing software downloaded from the Internet, emphasizing the need for the use of trusted application images available internally.

Special Action 1.5 Consider alternative sources of support

Consider your actions in a scenario where you are infected by malicious code that is not widely known, in which case you might not be able to obtain detailed information about the program from anti-virus vendors. Have contact information at hand for relevant mailing lists (see Resources) and user groups that you may need to query for containment and eradication information.

TYPE 2. PROBES AND NETWORK MAPPING

Probes are a special case of unauthorized access attempts. One class of probe occurs when a potential intruder uses an exploit script against your information systems, or firewall, and the script fails. The failure occurs because the exploit script does not find the target vulnerability. The probe then attempts to map your network using SNMP or broadcast ICMP "ping" packets to determine the architecture of your network. Another class of probe is used simply for information gathering. In this case, the attacker tests a variety of ports (a behavior often called a port scan), or host addresses (called a host scan), attempting to map your facility. Some attackers "war dial" your organization's phones looking for modems. With the widespread use of wireless networks, attackers are now "war driving" using wireless scanners like NetStumbler to find these networks.

Special Action 2.1 Report probes to your CIRT

Even if your facility doesn't have vulnerability, your customers and suppliers may. If they have access to your systems, your facility could still suffer. There is some controversy as to whether one should "bother" CIRTs by reporting probes. AusCERT's guidance on this follows: "A reason for reporting probes to your CIRT is that they act as a central reporting agency. We have seen cases of probes that were not considered significant by individual sites being part of significantly larger attacks against many sites."

Special Action 2.2 Assess the damage

It is great if the intruders do not actually get inside and do damage, but ask whether they learned information about your operating systems and network architecture that they can use in the future. Examine logs carefully; if the exploit script or technique is available, consider running it against yourself to determine what information can be learned.

TYPE 3. DENIAL OF SERVICE

Users rely on services provided by networks and computers. Attackers use many tools to cause your network and/or computer to cease operating effectively: erasing a critical program, "mail spamming and mail bombing" (flooding a user account with electronic mail), and altering system functionality by installing a Trojan horse program.

Special Action 3.1 (Advanced) Employ backups for core services

The most likely targets in your organization for a network attack are DNS, web and mail servers. If your organization conducts a lot of business over the Internet, it may pay to establish backup facilities. Denial of service attacks is a problem because they are hard to trace, easy to execute and they are effective. In such a dangerous environment, it is sometimes smart to use backups to bring the system back from a denial attack.

TYPE 4. INAPPROPRIATE USAGE

"Inappropriate usage" is the use of computer or network resources in a manner that violates an enterprise's policies or the law. Inappropriate usage ranges from theft of resources for personal gain or amusement to the use of resources to perpetrate crimes. By far the most common serious offense is the accessing, storing, or transmission of pornographic materials. Often, inappropriate usage investigations arise from an accusation that must be either proved or disproved by examination and analysis of the subject's work environment.

Special Action 4.1 Make certain your policy is sufficient for your investigation

Does it adequately inform the subjects of the investigation that they do not enjoy any assumption of privacy or personal ownership? Do the systems carry the necessary warning banners?

Special Action 4.2 Know the law

Make certain you know the laws for all jurisdictions. Since the investigation may involve multiple jurisdictions, the laws surrounding the examination of email and live transmissions can be quite difficult to ascertain quickly. Ignorance of federal and state wiretap laws does not constitute a viable legal defense. As the investigator, you are expected to know the laws relative to your profession. When in doubt, stop and consult your counsel.

Special Action 4.3 Consult with counsel

If any part of a request for information has directly or indirectly come from law enforcement, consult with your counsel. You may become an agent of the law enforcement agency and subject to additional laws restricting your ability to examine your enterprise's resources at will.

Special Action 4.4 Advise management of contingencies

Advise management at the outset that they may lose control of an investigation if the investigation reveals certain criminal activity. For example, if child pornography is uncovered, it must be reported and turned over to authorities. Authorities may elect to assume control of the investigation at that point.

Special Action 4.5 Analyze the risk of an investigation

Investigations carry many risks (privacy infringement claims, misinterpretation of investigative laws, errors of omission, intervention by authorities, etc.). If the only desire is to change behavior, and not to take an administrative action, there may be methods that are more efficient and present less risk than a resource intensive investigation.

Special Action 4.6 Establish legal protection

Since you do not know what will be uncovered, have the initiator of an investigation contact your enterprise's counsel before taking any action. One form of protection for you and your enterprise is the "Attorney Work Product" privilege. To maintain an attorney work product privilege, you must work on behalf of the attorney. Have the requests for investigative support come from the attorney to you, and return all information to the attorney alone.

Special Action 4.7 Keep the investigative team small, and maintain strict confidentiality

Inappropriate usage investigations present a risk of legal action. You are often dealing with accusations the subject may find embarrassing. Even if an individual is proven innocent of the accusations, rumors of an investigation can damage the individual's reputation and ability to function within the organization, as well as his standing in the community.

Special Action 4.8 Coordinate with physical security department

Failing to coordinate with your enterprise's physical security department when performing a subject work area investigation may inadvertently set off alarms or raise suspicions. Physical security may respond to what appears to be an unauthorized intrusion, possibly compromising the confidentiality of the investigation.

Special Action 4.9 Know your investigative team members

Make team assignments carefully. Some people become very distressed by some inappropriate materials (child pornography, death, torture and mutilation depictions). In non-law enforcement settings, many IT security members are computer or network specialists and may not be emotionally prepared to deal with these materials. Brief your team members on what to expect, and be ready to make assignment changes when requested or when you believe they're needed.

Special Action 4.10 Create a standardized presentation format

Inappropriate materials often create different emotions in the viewers. No two people seem to agree on how to define "obscenity".

Instead of presenting the materials directly, create a matrix that profiles the subject's involvement using a rating system (PG, R, X, XXX) versus activity (downloaded, stored, sent ...). This provides management and human resources with a tool for consistent administration of inappropriate usage cases without the need to show the actual materials.

Special Action 4.11 Create and use a retention policy for inappropriate usage, investigative case material

Use mandatory controlled storage for inappropriate materials collected in the course of an investigation, and destroy all copies as specified in the retention policy. Special care should be taken with materials considered to be contraband, such as child pornography. With any suspected contraband, follow the directions of your enterprise's counsel on an individual case basis.

TYPE 5. ESPIONAGE

Espionage is stealing information to subvert the interests of an organization or government. Many cases of unauthorized access to corporate systems are for espionage purposes.

Special Action 5.1 Maintain a very small core team

Espionage and insider criminal cases do not benefit from many helpers. The risk of an information leak or evidence contamination rises as additional workers are added to the investigation. A senior member of management such as the CIO, or Chief Security Officer must be advised as well as the incident handling team member on the legal staff. The technical lead should be one of the more seasoned members of the incident handling team, someone who has already proven capable in previous sensitive situations. One issue that often arises is whether to include the system administrator responsible for the system targeted in the attack. If you are reasonably sure the sysadmin is not involved in the espionage, the answer is probably yes.

Special Action 5.2 Maximize data collection

Ensure that access records of the affected facility are collected and protected. These may include records from badge access systems, phone records from your organization's PBX, log books, system logs, network logs and surveillance videos. Collect as much back data as possible.

Special Action 5.3 Consider mis-direction

If an outsider is collecting the information, you may be able to provide erroneous information and actually benefit from the incident. If you suspect the information is being collected and distributed by an insider, this is less likely to work.

Special Action 5.4 Target analysis

Review the lead or leads that tipped off the organization that they might be dealing with espionage. Ask what are the most probable targets of the activity. For each probable target, ask what the information is worth? Who (outside the organization) might benefit from having the information? What are all the possible ways to acquire these targets? What are the two or three most likely ways to acquire these targets? This process leads to a fairly simple, but important question: are monitoring capabilities in place for the most likely ways to acquire the most probable targets? If the answer is yes, begin reviewing the monitoring data immediately. If the answer is no, determine what is required to monitor the most likely ways to acquire the probable targets. Make it so.

Special Action 5.5 (Advanced) Establish a war room

A war room is a secure room with copies of evidence in the case. The purpose of a war room is to facilitate displaying the data in a meaningful way to help solve high risk or difficult cases. The walls of the room can be decorated with evidence, lines of investigation, charts from the target analysis process, maps of the area and blue prints of the facility. A tape player and TV/VCR should be available; it is often a good idea to record and play back interviews, or access tapes.

TYPE 6. HOAXES

WARNING: If you receive a mail message entitled "Here it is doodz" don't open it! If you do it will delete all the files on your hard disk, stop your pacemaker, and cause your dog to mess on the floor.

NOTE! In early 1995, hundreds of thousands of users with Internet access distributed information about a virus called the Good Times Virus, even though the virus did not exist. Hoaxes are valid incidents (remember, our definition of an incident included the threat of an adverse event). They tie up incident response resources as system administrators and incident handlers try to sort things out. Hoaxes also serve to make users uncomfortable with computing resources by spreading fear, uncertainty, and doubt.

Special Action 6.1 Use the Hoaxes page at CIAC (see Resources on page 61) to validate or debunk possible hoaxes

TYPE 7. UNAUTHORIZED ACCESS

Unauthorized access ranges from improperly logging into a user's account (e.g., when a hacker logs in to a legitimate user's account), to unauthorized access to files and directories stored on a system or storage media by obtaining superuser privileges. Unauthorized access could also entail access to additional computer systems facilitated by gathering logon names and passwords through an unauthorized "sniffer" program or device to capture all packets traversing the network at a particular point. Another common method used to gain unauthorized access is to exploit a vulnerability in information systems, routers, or even firewalls. Exploit scripts for gaining unauthorized access are widely available on hacker web sites.

Special Action 7.1 Examine firewall or filtering router protections

The single most likely avenue of attack from an outsider is through an organization's network connections, especially the Internet connection. If possible do not allow the "r-utilities", sunrpc, xwindows, or NetBIOS/IP. Telnet and FTP should be allowed only to systems that absolutely need to provide these services to the internet. Web, DNS servers and mail relay systems are always popular targets with attackers, run as few services on these systems as possible and ensure they are well protected.

Special Action 7.2 Regularly examine access services

It is not absolutely necessary to access another user's account to perpetrate an attack on a system or network. An intruder can access information, plant Trojan horse programs and so forth, by misusing available services. One example is outsiders using the network file system (NFS) or the file access mechanisms in Windows NT to reach files and directories in another of your organization's domain.

TYPE 8. INTELLECTUAL PROPERTY

Intellectual property (IP) includes the creative ideas and expressions of the human mind that possess commercial value and receive the legal protection of a property right. IP rights enable owners to select who may access and use their property, and to protect it from unauthorized use.

IP is a key value for many organizations. It is imperative that organizations protect their IP and are prepared to apply the incident handling process to intellectual property.

Prevention

Special Action 8.1 Inventory your intellectual property

Assign a person or department to regularly conduct and maintain an inventory of your organization's intellectual property (IP). The inventory should categorize the different types of IP (proprietary knowledge, trade secrets, patents, copyrights, trademarks, etc.) and be accessible only to those with a need to know. An organization must first know what it has in order to determine how to best protect it.

Special Action 8.2 Prioritize your intellectual property

Conduct regular risk assessments to identify your organization's critical IP. A risk assessment is a formal process that involves determining the probability that a given threat will exploit a particular vulnerability and the impact of the exploitation. Organizations may not be able to equally protect all of their IP. A well-done risk assessment will distinguish the crucial IP that must be strongly protected. Additionally, the risk assessment will enable organizations to respond appropriately to the misuse of specific IP. Misuse of critical IP should trigger a robust response while misuse of less critical IP may require less of a response.

Special Action 8.3 Assign financial value to your intellectual property

Regularly determine and document the value of your IP. The documentation should be accessible only by those with a need to know. Know how much it will cost your organization if specific IP is misused. If you have patents, franchises or copyrights for information you license, your organization will already have assigned a financial value to specific IP. Valuation of trade secrets should be based on the worth of cost savings, manufacturing efficiencies or strategic buying.

Knowing the value of IP is often necessary when discussing misuse incidents with law enforcement and when asking a court for damages. It is important to do this regularly as the value of certain IP may change over time.

Special Action 8.4 Uniquely identify your intellectual property

Use copyright notices, watermarks, or other forms of identification to uniquely identify your IP. Use methods that uniquely identify IP based on its distribution location or method. For instance, the SANS Step by Step books that are sold as .pdfs have a unique serial number embedded in them as well as other techniques that link the book to the purchasing organization. Carefully document this identification. Where possible, also create and securely store MD5 and SHA-1 signatures of your IP. These signatures can be used in the incident identification phase and be a part of detection methodologies.

Special Action 8.5 Implement intellectual property misuse detection methodologies

Conduct regular electronic and paper searches to discover misuse of your IP. Determine whether you have the necessary internal expertise to conduct such searches or need external assistance. A variety of commercial organizations provide customized IP searching services.

Special Action 8.6 Make it easy to report intellectual property misuse

Establish an easy method such as a 1-800 number, web form or email address for persons to report misuse of your organization's IP. Implement a formal, documented process for handling the reports, including thanking the person reporting the misuse. The person(s) who initially receives such reports should follow formal, documented procedures that define how the reports are to be managed. Organizations that receive many reports should establish a triage process that allows rapid identification of misuse of critical IP.

Special Action 8.7 Stay current with intellectual property laws

Carefully monitor and understand the IP laws in all the countries your organization does business in, not just your home country. An organization must have a clear and complete understanding of its rights in order to make effective decisions about how to protect its IP. Determine whether you have the necessary internal expertise to do this or need additional external help.

www.wipo.org/about-ip/en/ipworldwide provides detailed information about the IP laws of many different countries. www.cybercrime.gov is another useful source of information regarding IP laws.

Special Action 8.8 Implement legal protections for your intellectual property

Whenever possible, obtain patents, trademarks, copyrights, etc. for your IP. Implement the legal rights that apply to specific IP. Establish a formal, documented process for initially identifying IP, applying for IP protection and monitoring IP protection application status. Additionally, be sure to monitor the time frames for specific legal protections and reapply when appropriate (e.g. renewing a trademark).

Special Action 8.9 Establish an intellectual property management process

Implement a formal, documented process for the entire lifecycle of IP in your organization — IP creation, modification, storage, and distribution. This process will provide an overall framework, including policies, procedures, and specific cost effective security controls, for how your organization interacts with IP. The process should include clearly defined audit controls that carefully track and log IP, particularly its distribution.

Special Action 8.10 Establish an intellectual property policy

Establish and enforce a formal, documented policy that stresses to all employees the importance of protecting the organization's IP and the consequences of misusing IP. The policy might include the following requirements— use of the need to know principle, proper handling of trash, fax and copier controls, cleaning whiteboards at close of business, visitor management, file and document controls, sensitivity marking of documents, air gapped or segmented computer servers for critical information, and content screening on inbound and outbound internet traffic.

It is difficult for an organization to take action against an employee who misuses IP unless there is a formal policy that states what employees can and cannot do. The policy will also set a "tone" for your organization and may discourage some employees from misusing IP.

Special Action 8.11 Establish specific incident-response procedures for intellectual property misuse

Responding to misuse of your organization's IP will likely require a significantly different response than responding to other security incidents (e.g. denial of service or a compromised server). Create and maintain formal, documented procedures that are specifically for IP misuse incidents. The procedures should recognize that response will vary depending on where the IP misuse has occurred. For example, handling an IP misuse incident in the United States can require different actions than handling one in Bulgaria.

Special Action 8.12 Develop working relationships with your legal and public affairs staff

Responding to IP misuse can require organizations to take a variety of legal actions. BEFORE an IP misuse incident occurs, make sure your legal staff knows their role and that you understand their perspective and abilities. Know what IP expertise your internal legal staff has and when you'll need external proficiency. When possible, establish agreements with external lawyers that establish how quickly they must respond during an IP misuse incident.

Responding to IP misuse may also require your organization to conduct public relations (PR) activities. BEFORE an IP misuse incident occurs, your PR office should have and understand standardized information about the importance and requirements of IP in case they need to respond to a press query about an IP misuse incident. If your organization is a service provider, your PR office should also be familiar with the **Digital Millennium Copyright Act (DMCA)** safe harbor provisions.

Special Action 8.13 Develop working relationships with law enforcement

IP misuse response may require organizations to work with a variety of law enforcement agencies. BEFORE an IP misuse incident occurs, understand what types of IP misuse cases law enforcement will be interested in and how they will handle such cases. In general, law enforcement will not provide assistance unless the incident has caused significant financial damage to an organization.

Offer to educate local law enforcement on why it's important to protect IP and the methods your organization uses to protect its IP. Make sure you understand what information law enforcement will need to assist you.

Incident Identification and Response

Special Action 8.14 Thoroughly document identification of intellectual property misuse

Documentation of how misuse of your organization's IP is detected is critical. Proper documentation can spell success or failure in the courtroom. It can also assist in the identification of additional IP misuse. Additionally, careful documentation provides a blue print for others such as lawyers or law enforcement in the event they need to repeat the IP misuse identification.

Documentation should contain only facts. If you feel it is important to state opinions or assumptions, then clearly mark them as such within your documentation. This is particularly important when you create reports for legal, law enforcement, government or corporate officials.

Special Action 8.15 Check entire violator location for intellectual property misuse

Whether IP was found in a desk, workstation, web site or other place, check the entire location for other IP misuse. Try to keep this phase of the investigation as discrete as possible. If you are searching a web site, checking should be done offline with the use of offline browsing tools or the "cached" feature found on many search engines. It is important to identify all IP misuse as this will add to the total damage amount and can help persuade lawyers and law enforcement to take action.

When appropriate, also collect information on any violations of other organizations' IP you find. Notify the other IP owners of your findings and encourage them to take appropriate action. We must work together to protect our IP.

Special Action 8.16 Verify the authenticity and origin of the misused intellectual property

This will be fairly straightforward if you have identified your organization's IP through watermarks, content, or other mechanisms. It will be more challenging if you have not identified your IP or if a violator misuses portions of your IP within their own works.

There are numerous instances where violators have removed obvious copyright and trademark identifiers as well as removed the document's title in order to obscure its true owner. Thus, you may need to use multiple methods of authentication.

Special Action 8.17 Create a detected items log

This log will become the foundation of your evidence and may be necessary before you can receive assistance from lawyers or law enforcement. The log should include information such as IP type and locations such as a URL, filenames, timestamps, title, author, etc. When appropriate, include MD5 or SHA-1 signatures or the original and violated copies.

The Intellectual Property Incident Identification forms found at www.sans.org/incidentforms provide detailed examples of what information to collect.

Special Action 8.18 Assess the economic damage caused by intellectual property misuse

This will be much easier to do if your organization has already identified the base values of its IP. A key factor in determining damage will be how many times the IP has been misused by the violator.

For example, assume that a company that sells books in electronic form over the Internet has discovered that one of their best selling books is now being distributed for free on a violator's site. The economic damage caused by the misused version being downloaded one thousand times will be greater than if it has been downloaded only twice.

Special Action 8.19 Carefully collect and store evidence

Monitor and understand the current standards and techniques for digital evidence collection. Determine whether your organization has the necessary internal expertise or needs outside assistance or training. Questioning the "purity" and originality of digital evidence is a popular tactic of defense attorneys.

Perform all digital evidence gathering and analysis on bit-by-bit duplicates of the originals. Be sure to thoroughly document your collection procedures — when data was collected, what was collected, how it was collected and by whom. Properly identify each step you take. For example, if a screen shot is taken of a website containing IP misuse, you can immediately take an MD5 signature of that shot. To help maintain authenticity, be sure to keep the image creation time and MD5 creation time as close as possible together. Additionally, utilize offline browsing tools to capture a suspect's site at a specific point in time and write all evidence to media that cannot be modified, such as CD-R.

If you make an error during the collection process, do not panic. Thoroughly document the error and go on. Most importantly, try not to repeat the error again!

If in doubt, consult with your legal staff and appropriate law enforcement agencies on the proper evidence collection procedures for specific incidents.

Special Action 8.20 Gather appropriate information about intellectual property misusers

Utilize public sources to gather information on the violating individual or organization. Public sources include search engines, the violator's own website or storefront, publications, and public information databases. Information that should be collected includes names, locations, domain names, IP addresses, and contact information including phone numbers, email addresses, personal websites, and physical and mailing addresses. Always behave ethically and comply with all relevant laws while collecting evidence on a violator.

Special Action 8.21 Determine when to activate response teams

Every IP misuse incident may not justify a full response. Most organizations do not have unlimited resources or time to respond to IP misuse. Know what "battles" to fight. Such decisions are best made based on a risk assessment that identifies which IP is most important to your organization.

Special Action 8.22 Identify domain and ISP intellectual property protections

A significant number of ISPs and domain owners have strict IP and acceptable use policies. You can use this to your advantage if one of their customers is misusing your IP. Identify the owner of the network where the violation is occurring. Then make contact with them and describe the misuse. Many of them will then require the violator to remove the misused IP or have their web site taken down.

Additionally, some domains have dedicated DMCA agents for handling IP misuse; you will be able to direct all communications through that person. When you contact domain owners, ask them if they have a DMCA agent.

Special Action 8.23 Document all communications

Keep a log of all correspondence, phone calls, meetings, etc. that occur during an IP misuse incident. This will help identify liabilities that may exist once the final damage assessment is done. For example, if your requests to an ISP go ignored for months and during that time 1,000 more downloads of your misused IP occur, then a court may find the ISP liable for damages. Also, the individuals listed in the logs, such as DMCA agents and foreign law enforcement officials, may become key allies in future incidents. Keeping accurate and detailed notes of your communications also allows for quick retrieval of important facts as the need arises.

Containment

Special Action 8.24 Identify how intellectual property was inappropriately disclosed or used

This can be challenging and will be significantly based on your understanding of your organization's IP management process. For example, if the misused IP is private to your organization (e.g. trade secrets), then an employee may have leaked it or some other form of economic espionage may have occurred. However, misuse could also be due to lax permissions on your organization's website which allowed unauthorized persons to use and disclose your IP. Detailed forensics of a violator's system will usually reveal the most useful information; such access, however, will likely only be obtainable via a search warrant enforced by appropriate law enforcement.

When possible, identify and audit the actions of all persons who have interacted with the misused IP. In general this is only possible in small organizations or in larger organizations where only a small number of persons have interacted with specific IP. In such organizations, this can be an effective way to identify how IP was misused.

Once the reason for the IP misuse is identified, take appropriate steps to reduce or eliminate it.

Special Action 8.25 Verify that intellectual property distribution mechanisms are functioning properly

Make sure that trusted third parties or resellers of your IP have not been compromised. For example, assume your organization is a producer of electronic books and it partners with only one online company to resell them. If you find your books are being misused, you should contact the partner company to make sure that they have not been compromised. They also may be able to match a violator's Internet Protocol address or email address to an entry in their download logs.

Eradication

Special Action 8.26 Review and update detection schemes and intellectual property management process

Utilize the information gathered during the identification and containment phases of an incident and use it to update and improve your policies, procedures and controls. This will help in preventing and responding to future IP misuse.

Special Action 8.27 Regularly check previously exploited vulnerabilities

If an IP misuse incident was caused by the exploitation of a specific vulnerability, regularly check to make sure that the vulnerability remains secured. If the incident was due to a breakdown or inadequacy in your organization's IP management process, establish careful auditing of appropriate IP management events.

Special Action 8.28 Regularly check previous intellectual property misuse web sites.

Once it has been verified that your misused IP has been removed from a web site, be sure that the violator does not simply place the IP in another location on the web site, rename it, or repost it later. Also, if a violator's ISP shuts down their website, the violator may immediately acquire a new site with a different ISP and continue to misuse your IP. Conduct regular electronic searches or use a commercial IP searching company to detect these "repeat "offenders.

Recovery

Special Action 8.29 Keep the recovery team informed

A very significant IP misuse incident or repeated incidents over a long period of time may require an organization to recover its IP. A recovery team will likely be formed. This team will need to be kept well informed about all IP misuse incidents that could significantly impact the organization's image or profits.

INCIDENT RECORD KEEPING

Record keeping is crucial for each of the six phases of incident handling above. Use a log book to record the nature of suspicious events immediately after they've been observed. Include the name of the system, time, and other details related to the observations, even details that may not seem to be very relevant at the time they're recorded. Also, record the names of those with whom you discussed the incident or possible incident. Careful recording of these details can assist efforts to identify the nature of an incident, develop effective solutions, and prosecute those who commit computer crime.

Conventional wisdom among incident handlers is to use a new bound blank book such as those commonly available at "dollar stores". Other folks prefer spiral bound notebooks. Either option is fine. Just be sure that you take notes that you would be proud to see displayed in a courtroom six months later. That means never doodle or write sarcastic remarks in your notebook!

Video and audio recordings of the event provide an excellent record of what transpires, and may be very useful in court. However, they may collect more information about your organization's structure and specific facts that you do not wish to reveal. If you do use these tools, you may be forced to turn them all over in a legal situation. Discuss the use of these tools with your attorney before you actually use them in an incident.

Experienced incident handlers rarely need more than three or four pages to record most of the essential information. However, the pace of incident handling is very fast, so remembering what to record may become difficult.

In this Step-by-Step guide, we provide forms you may use as an alternative option to notebooks. Or you may use them as aids to help you remember what to record in the notebooks. The forms will prompt you to record information that might be useful to you as your memory begins to dim. Feel free to reproduce them and give them a try during a mock incident to see what works well for you. There are two different sets of forms. The first set is for computer security incidents. The second set is for intellectual property incidents. Both sets are posted at www.sans.org/incidentforms/ and as always we are interested in your feedback on ways to improve them. Whether you use the forms, notebooks, or a combination, remember to sign, date, and number the pages you use, and store them in an "evidence worthy" container.

The Command Post Team members must also make sure that they keep an accurate record of the information that they receive from the On Site Team, as well as any communications to individuals outside the CIRT team, such as executives or local law enforcement officials. If the managers on the Command Team have an excellent working relationship with their secretaries or administrative assistants, your organization may benefit by having these employees on the Command Post Team.

Definitions of incidents and events

Incident

The term "incident" refers to an adverse event in an information system, and/or network, or the threat of the occurrence of such an event. Examples of incidents include unauthorized use of another user's account, unauthorized use of system privileges, and execution of malicious code that destroys data. Incident implies harm, or the attempt to harm.

Event

An "event" is any observable occurrence in a system and/or network. Examples of events include the system boot sequence, a system crash, and packet flooding within a network. These observable events recorded in the incident-handling notebook, along with the evidence you are able to collect, provide the bulk of your organization's case if the perpetrator of an incident is caught and prosecuted.

COMPUTER SECURITY INCIDENT CONTACT LIST DATE: ______________ PAGE ___ OF ___

Security Officer:

Name: ______________________________
Title: ______________________________
Phone: ____________ Alt. Phone: ____________
Mobile: ____________ Pager: ____________
Fax: ____________ Alt. Fax: ____________
E-mail: ______________________________
Address: ______________________________
____

Incident Handling, CIRT, or FIRST Team:

Name: ______________________________
Title: ______________________________
Phone: ____________ Alt. Phone: ____________
Mobile: ____________ Pager: ____________
Fax: ____________ Alt. Fax: ____________
E-mail: ______________________________
Address: ______________________________
____

Legal Affairs Officer:

Name: ______________________________
Title: ______________________________
Phone: ____________ Alt. Phone: ____________
Mobile: ____________ Pager: ____________
Fax: ____________ Alt. Fax: ____________
E-mail: ______________________________
Address: ______________________________
____

CIO or Information Systems Security Manager:

Name: ______________________________
Title: ______________________________
Phone: ____________ Alt. Phone: ____________
Mobile: ____________ Pager: ____________
Fax: ____________ Alt. Fax: ____________
E-mail: ______________________________
Address: ______________________________
____

Public Affairs Officer:

Name: ______________________________
Title: ______________________________
Phone: ____________ Alt. Phone: ____________
Mobile: ____________ Pager: ____________
Fax: ____________ Alt. Fax: ____________
E-mail: ______________________________
Address: ______________________________
____

Other (Specify): ______________________

Name: ______________________________
Title: ______________________________
Phone: ____________ Alt. Phone: ____________
Mobile: ____________ Pager: ____________
Fax: ____________ Alt. Fax: ____________
E-mail: ______________________________
Address: ______________________________
____

COMPUTER SECURITY INCIDENT CONTACT LIST

DATE: ______________ **PAGE** ___ **OF** ___

Internet Service Provider Technical Contact:

Name: ____________________
Title: ____________________
Phone: __________ Alt. Phone: __________
Mobile: __________ Pager: __________
Fax: __________ Alt. Fax: __________
E-mail: ____________________
Address: ____________________
____

Local FBI or Equivalent Agency:

Name: ____________________
Title: ____________________
Phone: __________ Alt. Phone: __________
Mobile: __________ Pager: __________
Fax: __________ Alt. Fax: __________
E-mail: ____________________
Address: ____________________
____

Local Law Enforcement Computer Crime:

Name: ____________________
Title: ____________________
Phone: __________ Alt. Phone: __________
Mobile: __________ Pager: __________
Fax: __________ Alt. Fax: __________
E-mail: ____________________
Address: ____________________
____

Local CIRT or FIRST Team:

Name: ____________________
Title: ____________________
Phone: __________ Alt. Phone: __________
Mobile: __________ Pager: __________
Fax: __________ Alt. Fax: __________
E-mail: ____________________
Address: ____________________
____

Other (Specify):____________________

Name: ____________________
Title: ____________________
Phone: __________ Alt. Phone: __________
Mobile: __________ Pager: __________
Fax: __________ Alt. Fax: __________
E-mail: ____________________
Address: ____________________
____

Other (Specify):____________________

Name: ____________________
Title: ____________________
Phone: __________ Alt. Phone: __________
Mobile: __________ Pager: __________
Fax: __________ Alt. Fax: __________
E-mail: ____________________
Address: ____________________
____

COMPUTER SECURITY INCIDENT IDENTIFICATION

DATE: ______________ PAGE ___ OF ___

General Information

Incident Detector's Information:

Name: ______________________________ Date and Time Detected: ____________________

Title: ______________________________

Phone: ____________ Alt. Phone: ____________ Location Incident Detected From: ____________________

Mobile: ____________ Pager: ____________ ______________________________

Fax: ____________ Alt. Fax: ____________ Additional Information: ____________________

E-mail: ____

Address: ____

____

Detector's Signature: ______________________ Date Signed: ______________________

Incident Summary

Type of Incident Detected:

__Denial of Service __ Unauthorized Use __ Espionage __ Probe __ Hoax

__ Malicious Code __ Unauthorized Access __ Other: ______________________

Incident Location:

Site: ______________________________ How was the Intellectual Property Detected: ________

Site Point of Contact: ______________________ ______________________________

Phone: ____________ Alt. Phone: ____________ ______________________________

Mobile: ____________ Pager: ____________ ______________________________

Fax: ____________ Alt. Fax: ____________ ______________________________

E-mail: ______________________________ ______________________________

Address: ______________________________ ______________________________

______________________________ ______________________________

Additional Information: ____

____

____

COMPUTER SECURITY INCIDENT SURVEY **DATE: ________ PAGE ___ OF ___**

Location(s) of affected systems: ______________________________

____

____

____

Date and time incident handlers arrived at site: ______________________________

____

____

Describe affected information system(s) (one form per system is recommended):

Hardware Manufacturer: ______________________________

Serial Number: ______________________________

Corporate Property Number (if applicable): ______________________________

Is the affected system connected to a modem? __YES __NO

System Name: ______________________________

System Network Address: ______________________________

MAC Address: ______________________________

Is the affected system connected to a modem? __YES __NO

Phone Number: ______________________________

Describe the physical security of the location of affected information systems (locks, security alarms, building access, etcetera):

____

____

____

____

____

____

COMPUTER SECURITY INCIDENT CONTAINMENT

DATE: ________ PAGE ___ OF ___

Isolate affected systems:

Command Decision Team approved removal from network? __YES __NO

If YES, date and time systems were removed: ______________________________

If NO, state the reason: ______________________________

____

____

Backup affected systems:

System backup successful for all systems? __YES __NO

Name of persons who did backup: ______________________________

____

____

____

____

Date and time backups started: ______________________________

Date and time backups complete: ______________________________

Backup tapes sealed? __YES __NO Seal Date: ______________________________

Backup tapes turned over to: ______________________________

Signature: ______________________________ Date: ______________

Backup Storage Location: ______________________________

COMPUTER SECURITY INCIDENT ERADICATION **DATE: ________ PAGE ___ OF ___**

Name of persons performing forensics on systems: ____

____

____

____

____

Was the vulnerability identified? __ YES __NO

Describe: ____

____

____

____

____

____

What was the validation procedure used to ensure problem was eradicated: ____________________

____

____

____

____

____

____

____

INCIDENT COMMUNICATION LOG **DATE: ________ PAGE ___ OF ___**

Date: ____________ **Time:** ________ __ **am** __**pm** **Method (mail, phone, email, etc.):** ____________
Initiator Name: ______________________ Receiver Name: ______________________
Initiator Title: ______________________ Receiver Title: ______________________
Initiator Organization: ______________________ Receiver Organization: ______________________
Initiator Contact Info: ______________________ Receiver Contact Info: ______________________
Details: ____

Date: ____________ **Time:** ________ __ **am** __**pm** **Method (mail, phone, email, etc.):** ____________
Initiator Name: ______________________ Receiver Name: ______________________
Initiator Title: ______________________ Receiver Title: ______________________
Initiator Organization: ______________________ Receiver Organization: ______________________
Initiator Contact Info: ______________________ Receiver Contact Info: ______________________
Details: ____

Date: ____________ **Time:** ________ __ **am** __**pm** **Method (mail, phone, email, etc.):** ____________
Initiator Name: ______________________ Receiver Name: ______________________
Initiator Title: ______________________ Receiver Title: ______________________
Initiator Organization: ______________________ Receiver Organization: ______________________
Initiator Contact Info: ______________________ Receiver Contact Info: ______________________
Details: ____

INTELLECTUAL PROPERTY INCIDENT CONTACT LIST **DATE: ________ PAGE ___ OF ___**

Intellectual Property (IP) Owner Contacts

Security Officer:

Name: ______________________________
Title: ______________________________
Phone: ____________ Alt. Phone: ____________
Mobile: ____________ Pager: ____________
Fax: ____________ Alt. Fax: ____________
E-mail: ______________________________
Address: ______________________________
____

Incident Handling, CIRT, or FIRST Team:

Name: ______________________________
Title: ______________________________
Phone: ____________ Alt. Phone: ____________
Mobile: ____________ Pager: ____________
Fax: ____________ Alt. Fax: ____________
E-mail: ______________________________
Address: ______________________________
____

DMCA Agent:

Name: ______________________________
Title: ______________________________
Phone: ____________ Alt. Phone: ____________
Mobile: ____________ Pager: ____________
Fax: ____________ Alt. Fax: ____________
E-mail: ______________________________
Address: ______________________________
____

CIO or Information Systems Security Manager:

Name: ______________________________
Title: ______________________________
Phone: ____________ Alt. Phone: ____________
Mobile: ____________ Pager: ____________
Fax: ____________ Alt. Fax: ____________
E-mail: ______________________________
Address: ______________________________
____

Public Affairs Officer:

Name: ______________________________
Title: ______________________________
Phone: ____________ Alt. Phone: ____________
Mobile: ____________ Pager: ____________
Fax: ____________ Alt. Fax: ____________
E-mail: ______________________________
Address: ______________________________
____

Legal Affairs Officer

Name: ______________________________
Title: ______________________________
Phone: ____________ Alt. Phone: ____________
Mobile: ____________ Pager: ____________
Fax: ____________ Alt. Fax: ____________
E-mail: ______________________________
Address: ______________________________
____

INTELLECTUAL PROPERTY INCIDENT CONTACT LIST

DATE: ________ PAGE ___ OF ___

IP Owner Local Contacts

Internet Service Provider Technical Contact:

Name: ______________________________
Title: ______________________________
Phone: ____________ Alt. Phone: ____________
Mobile: ____________ Pager: ____________
Fax: ____________ Alt. Fax: ____________
E-mail: ______________________________
Address: ______________________________
____

Local FBI or Equivalent Agency:

Name: ______________________________
Title: ______________________________
Phone: ____________ Alt. Phone: ____________
Mobile: ____________ Pager: ____________
Fax: ____________ Alt. Fax: ____________
E-mail: ______________________________
Address: ______________________________
____

Local Law Enforcement Computer Crime:

Name: ______________________________
Title: ______________________________
Phone: ____________ Alt. Phone: ____________
Mobile: ____________ Pager: ____________
Fax: ____________ Alt. Fax: ____________
E-mail: ______________________________
Address: ______________________________
____

Local CIRT or FIRST Team:

Name: ______________________________
Title: ______________________________
Phone: ____________ Alt. Phone: ____________
Mobile: ____________ Pager: ____________
Fax: ____________ Alt. Fax: ____________
E-mail: ______________________________
Address: ______________________________
____

Other (Specify):

Name: ______________________________
Title: ______________________________
Phone: ____________ Alt. Phone: ____________
Mobile: ____________ Pager: ____________
Fax: ____________ Alt. Fax: ____________
E-mail: ______________________________
Address: ______________________________
____

Other (Specify):

Name: ______________________________
Title: ______________________________
Phone: ____________ Alt. Phone: ____________
Mobile: ____________ Pager: ____________
Fax: ____________ Alt. Fax: ____________
E-mail: ______________________________
Address: ______________________________
____

INTELLECTUAL PROPERTY INCIDENT CONTACT LIST

DATE: ________ PAGE ___ OF ___

Suspect's Local Contacts

Suspect's Internet Service Provider (ISP)

Technical Contact:

Name: ______________________________
Title: ______________________________
Phone: ____________ Alt. Phone: ____________
Mobile: ____________ Pager: ____________
Fax: ____________ Alt. Fax: ____________
E-mail: ______________________________
Address: ______________________________
____

Suspect's ISP DMCA Agent:

Name: ______________________________
Title: ______________________________
Phone: ____________ Alt. Phone: ____________
Mobile: ____________ Pager: ____________
Fax: ____________ Alt. Fax: ____________
E-mail: ______________________________
Address: ______________________________
____

Suspect's Local FBI or Equivalent Agency:

Name: ______________________________
Title: ______________________________
Phone: ____________ Alt. Phone: ____________
Mobile: ____________ Pager: ____________
Fax: ____________ Alt. Fax: ____________
E-mail: ______________________________
Address: ______________________________
____

Suspect's Local Law Enforcement Computer Crime:

Name: ______________________________
Title: ______________________________
Phone: ____________ Alt. Phone: ____________
Mobile: ____________ Pager: ____________
Fax: ____________ Alt. Fax: ____________
E-mail: ______________________________
Address: ______________________________
____

Suspect's Local CIRT or FIRST Team:

Name: ______________________________
Title: ______________________________
Phone: ____________ Alt. Phone: ____________
Mobile: ____________ Pager: ____________
Fax: ____________ Alt. Fax: ____________
E-mail: ______________________________
Address: ______________________________
____

Other (Specify):

Name: ______________________________
Title: ______________________________
Phone: ____________ Alt. Phone: ____________
Mobile: ____________ Pager: ____________
Fax: ____________ Alt. Fax: ____________
E-mail: ______________________________
Address: ______________________________
____

INTELLECTUAL PROPERTY INCIDENT CONTACT LIST

DATE: ________ PAGE ___ OF ___

Suspect's Local Contacts

Suspect's Web Hosting Technical Contact:

Name: ____________________
Title: ____________________
Phone: __________ Alt. Phone: __________
Mobile: __________ Pager: __________
Fax: __________ Alt. Fax: __________
E-mail: ____________________
Address: ____________________
____

Suspect's Web Hosting DMCA Agent:

Name: ____________________
Title: ____________________
Phone: __________ Alt. Phone: __________
Mobile: __________ Pager: __________
Fax: __________ Alt. Fax: __________
E-mail: ____________________
Address: ____________________
____

Other (Specify): ____________________

Name: ____________________
Title: ____________________
Phone: __________ Alt. Phone: __________
Mobile: __________ Pager: __________
Fax: __________ Alt. Fax: __________
E-mail: ____________________
Address: ____________________
____

Other (Specify): ____________________

Name: ____________________
Title: ____________________
Phone: __________ Alt. Phone: __________
Mobile: __________ Pager: __________
Fax: __________ Alt. Fax: __________
E-mail: ____________________
Address: ____________________
____

Other (Specify): ____________________

Name: ____________________
Title: ____________________
Phone: __________ Alt. Phone: __________
Mobile: __________ Pager: __________
Fax: __________ Alt. Fax: __________
E-mail: ____________________
Address: ____________________
____

Other (Specify): ____________________

Name: ____________________
Title: ____________________
Phone: __________ Alt. Phone: __________
Mobile: __________ Pager: __________
Fax: __________ Alt. Fax: __________
E-mail: ____________________
Address: ____________________
____

INTELLECTUAL PROPERTY INCIDENT CONTACT LIST

DATE: ________ PAGE ___ OF ___

Suspect's Contacts

Suspect Individual:

Name: ______________________________
Title: ______________________________
Phone: ____________ Alt. Phone: ____________
Mobile: ____________ Pager: ____________
Fax: ____________ Alt. Fax: ____________
E-mail: ______________________________
Address: ______________________________
____

Suspect Organization:

Name: ______________________________
Title: ______________________________
Phone: ____________ Alt. Phone: ____________
Mobile: ____________ Pager: ____________
Fax: ____________ Alt. Fax: ____________
E-mail: ______________________________
Address: ______________________________
____

Suspect Technical Contact:

Name: ______________________________
Title: ______________________________
Phone: ____________ Alt. Phone: ____________
Mobile: ____________ Pager: ____________
Fax: ____________ Alt. Fax: ____________
E-mail: ______________________________
Address: ______________________________
____

Suspect DMCA Agent:

Name: ______________________________
Title: ______________________________
Phone: ____________ Alt. Phone: ____________
Mobile: ____________ Pager: ____________
Fax: ____________ Alt. Fax: ____________
E-mail: ______________________________
Address: ______________________________
____

Suspect Legal Contact:

Name: ______________________________
Title: ______________________________
Phone: ____________ Alt. Phone: ____________
Mobile: ____________ Pager: ____________
Fax: ____________ Alt. Fax: ____________
E-mail: ______________________________
Address: ______________________________
____

Other (Specify): ______________________________

Name: ______________________________
Title: ______________________________
Phone: ____________ Alt. Phone: ____________
Mobile: ____________ Pager: ____________
Fax: ____________ Alt. Fax: ____________
E-mail: ______________________________
Address: ______________________________
____

INTELLECTUAL PROPERTY INCIDENT IDENTIFICATION DATE: ________ PAGE ___ OF ___

General Information

Incident Detector's Information:

Name: ____________________ Date and Time Detected: ____________________

Title: ____________________

Phone: __________ Alt. Phone: __________ Location Incident Detected From: ____________________

Mobile: __________ Pager: __________ ____________________

Fax: __________ Alt. Fax: __________ Additional Information: ____________________

E-mail: ____________________ ____________________

Address: ____________________ ____________________

____________________ ____________________

Detector's Signature: ____________________ Date Signed: ____________________

Intellectual Property Profile Summary

Type of Intellectual Property (IP) Detected: __________ Total Number of IP Items Detected: __________

__Document(s) __ Audio __Application(s)__ Image(s) __Video Additional Information: __________

Other: ____________________

Root Location of IP Items (URL, etc) on Detected System: ____________________

____

How was the Intellectual Property Detected: ____________________

____

____

____

____

____

____

____

____

____

INTELLECTUAL PROPERTY INCIDENT IDENTIFICATION DATE: ________ PAGE ___ OF ___

Intellectual Property Profile Detail – Detected Items Log

IP Item Number: ____________________ **File Type:** __________ **Size:** __________
Filename: ____________________ Time Stamp: __________ Version: __________
Detected File Location (URL, etc.): ____________________
Original File Location (URL, etc.): ____________________
Title: ____________________ Copyright: ____________________
Author: ____________________ Author E-mail: ____________________
Publisher: ____________________ Publish Date: ____________________
Company: ____________________ Company E-mail: ____________________
Company Address: ____________________ Company Phone: __________ Fax: __________
Additional Information: ____________________
____

IP Item Number: ____________________ **File Type:** __________ **Size:** __________
Filename: ____________________ Time Stamp: __________ Version: __________
Detected File Location (URL, etc.): ____________________
Original File Location (URL, etc.): ____________________
Title: ____________________ Copyright: ____________________
Author: ____________________ Author E-mail: ____________________
Publisher: ____________________ Publish Date: ____________________
Company: ____________________ Company E-mail: ____________________
Company Address: ____________________ Company Phone: __________ Fax: __________
Additional Information: ____________________
____

INTELLECTUAL PROPERTY INCIDENT CONTAINMENT DATE: ________ PAGE ___ OF ___

How were the intellectual property items compromised:

Are the original files accessible from company resources? __YES __NO
If YES, properly document location(s) on the Incident Identification form.

Are the original files secured? __YES __NO
If YES, how and where are these files secured: ______________________________

Have the company systems been reviewed for possible authorized or unauthorized access? __YES __NO
If YES, where is the location of the report or incident handling forms documenting this access: ______________________________
____

If NO, what was the reason: ______________________________
____

Have trusted partner systems been reviewed for possible authorized or unauthorized access? __YES __NO
If YES, where is the location of the report or incident handling forms documenting this access: ______________________________
____

If NO, what was the reason: ______________________________
____

Are the trusted partner system files secured? __YES __NO
If YES, how and where are these files secured: ______________________________
____

If NO, what was the reason: ______________________________
____

List other known authorized and unauthorized mechanisms of file distribution and possible usage or exploitation:
____
____
____
____

INTELLECTUAL PROPERTY INCIDENT ERADICATION DATE: ________ PAGE ___ OF ___

Names and Contact information of all people performing forensic and investigational duties:

____

____

____

____

____

____

____

Was the vulnerability identified?__YES __NO

If YES, describe: ____

____

____

____

Was the vulnerability eradicated? __YES __NO

If YES, describe: ____

____

____

____

____

What were the validation procedures used to ensure the problem was eradicated: ____________

____

____

____

____

____

INCIDENT FOLLOW-UP AND LESSONS LEARNED

Below you will find some suggested questions for the Lessons Learned meeting.

The primary purpose of the meeting is to improve your incident handling process, not to play politics! In almost every incident some things are done well, some things aren't. People have a tendency to remember the screw-ups. Accentuate the positive.

The questions below are to be answered by the incident handling team. All affected parties are welcome to comment.

Briefly describe what has transpired and what was done to intervene. Was there sufficient preparation for the incident? What preparation wasn't done that should have been done?

- **Did detection occur promptly or, if not, why not?**
- **What additional tools could have helped the detection and eradication process?**
- **Was the incident sufficiently contained?**
- **Was communication adequate, or could it have been better?**

We have never been involved in a serious incident where anyone could seriously claim that "communication was great". The phone lines are overtaxed; the onsite team has trouble reaching the command decision team to provide them needed tactical information. As stress goes up, communication degrades. The point of this question is to find ways to improve communication. An organization might not wish to approve three extra phone lines into the facility that will be used by the command decision team. After an incident, (and its lessons learned phase), in which the team was unable to stay in communication with critical parts of the organization, phone lines are often installed without further comment.

- **What practical difficulties were encountered?**

Analyzing the cost of the incident. Work within your chain of command to determine personnel time that was invested in dealing with the incident, including time necessary to restore systems. Convert those hours into monetary cost. The simplest method is to multiply the time spent by the burdened rate, usually about 1.5 times what the organization pays in salary.

- **Ask how much the incident disrupted ongoing operations?**
- **Were any data irrecoverably lost, and, if so, what was the value of the data?**
- **Was any hardware damaged?**

Generate an executive summary that includes cost and schedule impacts. If possible, post the results of the incident investigation on the incident handling intranet web page.

RESOURCES SUGGESTED BY THE CONTRIBUTORS

Web sites

Incidents.Org monitors the web daily and provides continuous information about ongoing attack patterns.
www.incidents.org

AusCERT posts advisories and also has information about security tools.
www.auscert.org.au/

The ***Computer Emergency Response Center*** posts advisories and also has information on recovering from an intrusion.
www.cert.org/
ftp.cert.org/pub/incident_reporting_form

The ***Computer Incident Advisory Capability*** posts advisories, has sections on hoaxes, chain letters, viruses and other security resources.
www.ciac.org/ciac/

The ***Forum of Incident Response and Security Teams*** web site can help you locate your CIRT team.
www.first.org

The High Tech Crime Investigation Association has regional sub groups that may be beneficial.
htcia.org

Kumite has a section on virus myths and hoaxes.
www.kumite.com

Rootshell and sabotage have collections of exploits.
www.rootshell.com
www.sabotage.org/rootshell/

Site Security Handbook, RFC 2196
ftp.isi.edu/in-notes/rfc2196.txt

Federal Cyber Crime informational site
www.cybercrime.gov

Good licensing guidelines
legal.web.aol.com/ip/ipguide/licensin.html

U.S. Patent & Trademark Office
www.uspto.gov

United States Copyright Office
lcweb.loc.gov/copyright/

Copyright Act
www4.law.cornell.edu/uscode/17/

The ***Trademark Anti-Dilution Act***
www4.law.cornell.edu/uscode/15/

Sonny Bono Copyright Term Extension Act
www.loc.gov/copyright/legislation/s505.pdf

Universal Copyright Convention (UCC)
www.unesco.org/culture/laws/copyright/html_eng/page1.shtml

Berne Convention for the Protection of Literary and Artistic Works
www.law.cornell.edu/treaties/berne/overview.html

Community Trademarks in the European Union
www.gigalaw.com/articles/2000-all/yu-2000-11-all.html

World Intellectual Property Organization
www.wipo.org/index.html.en

Madrid System for the International Registration of Marks
www.wipo.org/madrid/en/

Economic Espionage Act of 1996
www.scip.org/Library/8(3)eea.pdf

Anticybersquatting Consumer Protection Act
www.uspto.gov/web/offices/com/speeches/h1554gb1.pdf

The ***Digital Millennium Copyright Act of 1998***
www.loc.gov/copyright/legislation/dmca.pdf

Mailing List

The ***Security Alert Consensus*** mailing list is an authoritative source of vulnerability information that is often posted long before traditional advisories. To subscribe www.sans.org/newlook/digests/SAC.htm

Digests

The ***SANS Newsbites*** with the assistance of the half-dozen top security experts in the US, summarizes the twenty top security news stories each week. Email digest@sans.org with the subject "Subscribe Newsbites".

The ***Windows Security Digest*** offers authoritative information monthly about new threats to Windows systems and how to block them. Email digest@sans.org with the subject "Subscribe Windows Digest".